# Watercolour
## Still Lifes

# Watercolour
## Still Lifes

## Projects, Tips and Techniques

General Editor: Richard Taylor

amber
BOOKS

First published in 2006 by
Amber Books Ltd
Bradley's Close
74-77 White Lion Street
London N1 9PF
www.amberbooks.co.uk

© 2006 DeAgostini UK Ltd

ISBN-13: 978-1-904687-72-6
ISBN-10: 1-904687-72-5

Distributed in the UK by
Bookmart Ltd
Blaby Road
Wigston
Leicester LE18 4SE

**Contributing Artists:**
Mike Clark: 81–84; Abi Edgar: 56–61; Shirley Feltz: 24–30;
Sharon Finmark: 18–23; Lavinia Hamer: 91–96; Ian McCaughrean:
39–45; John Raynes: 85–90; Ian Sidaway: 31–38; Tig Sutton: 6–17,
62–67; Richard Taylor: 46–51; Jane Telford: 75–80; Paul Velarde:
68–74; Albany Wiseman: 52–55

**Picture Credits:**
DeAgostini/George Taylor

Printed in Singapore

# Contents

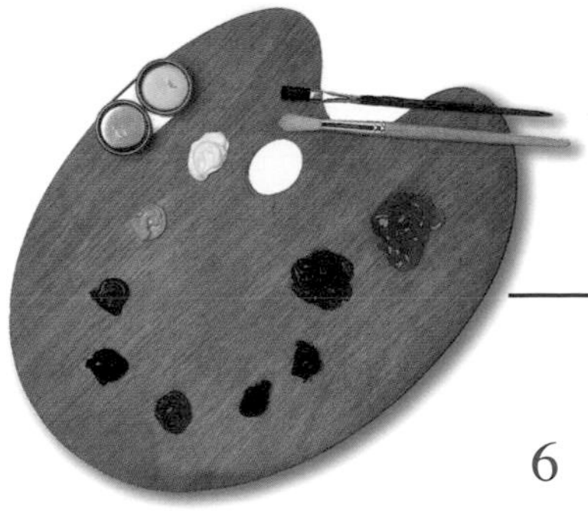

Still life with pumpkins     6

Bowl of eggs     12

Statue in watercolour     18

Sunflowers and bamboo leaves     24

A lemon, a pear and an orange     31

Orange lilies     39

Watercolour crab     46

Still life with peppers     52

Shiny copper and glass     56

Coffee and croissants     62

Brilliant anemones     68

Birman temple cat     75

Potted hyacinths     81

Still life with melon     85

Trout in watercolour     91

# Still life with pumpkins

*A tinted paper will give your watercolour a ready-made, even undertone and impose a pleasing sense of harmony.*

◄ The biscuit colour of the paper chosen for this still life harmonizes well with the warm tones of the apples, pumpkins, flagon and pitcher.

One of the advantages of still life is the degree of control you have over the subject. You can choose objects for their shape, colour or texture, select them for their similarities or for their differences, and arrange and light them as you wish. An important aspect of the initial decision-making process is choosing the paper you want to work on, as this plays its part in creating the mood of the painting.

Pure watercolour is a translucent medium which relies on the white or off-white of the paper to provide the lightest tone. Lightly tinted papers can be very effective with watercolour, but you should choose the colour carefully.

A tinted paper has several advantages. It is less stark and therefore less daunting than starting with a pure white ground. It also serves as a key against which to judge other tones and provides a background colour to the whole painting, creating a sense of unity.

When choosing a tinted paper, find one that echoes a dominant colour in the set-up, or choose a colour to create a mood. Alternatively, you can tint your own paper by laying a flat wash over it.

### 'Drawing' with watercolour

For this still-life project, the artist has dispensed with an initial pencil drawing. The main forms of the two pumpkins, the basket and the pottery

items have been established with a thin wash of burnt sienna and burnt umber. If you use this direct method of working, you will find that it will give your painting a pleasingly spontaneous feel as you progress through the stages.

Don't worry if you make a few mistakes while you are outlining the objects or blocking in the tones. As long as you use a pale wash, the redrawn lines will disappear beneath the subsequent washes. Do be careful, however, to reserve the areas of lightest tone, such as the basket and the body of the flagon.

▼ **Mix permanent rose and burnt sienna for a good terra-cotta shade.**

## EXPERT ADVICE
### Creating highlights on tinted paper

If you are using watercolour on a tinted paper, you may find that you need some highlights to give the image a complete range of tones. If the paper is not pale enough to provide these brilliant touches, you will have to introduce them by using white paint. Chinese white is a zinc white paint specially prepared for use with watercolour and can be added sparingly to a painting to great effect.

### FIRST STROKES

**1** ▼ **Start blocking in the tones** Mix a dilute wash of burnt sienna and burnt umber. Using a No. 6 brush, start to block in the broad forms of the subject on tinted paper, looking for areas of dark and mid tone. If you half-close your eyes, you will be able to see the lights and darks more clearly.

**2** ▲ **Continue establishing the main tones** Add more burnt umber to the wash and lay in the shaded areas between the objects. Keep the wash very pale so that you can paint over any mistakes. Note the way the tones of the objects change as the surfaces curve away from the light source.

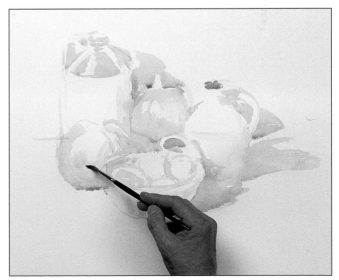

**3** ▲ **Block in the pumpkins** Using a wash of cadmium yellow deep with a touch of scarlet, establish the broad forms of the pumpkins. Leave highlights as bare paper. Stand back and check the proportions of the objects, making any necessary adjustment by overpainting.

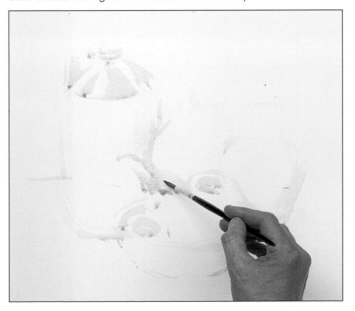

**4** ▼ **Start to lay in the background** Mix a pale wash of raw sienna, light red and burnt umber, and use it for the body of the pitcher and the shadows on the wall. Apply the same wash as horizontal slabs of colour to suggest the pattern of the tiled surface. Allow the painting to dry thoroughly at this stage.

**5** ▶ **Build up the mid and dark tones** Dark tones can be created by overlaying several thin layers of wash. Here, the convex surface of the pitcher is suggested by laying another wash over the right side and along the lower part where the body curves away from the light source. Notice the two curved lines, which suggest the ribbed surface of the pot.

**6** ◀ **Add areas of dark shadow** With a darker wash of raw umber and light red, paint the shadow behind the pumpkin at the back, defining an accurate silhouette. Now use the same mix to create the important shadow under the handle of the pitcher. Add bands of the wash around the pumpkin in the foreground to suggest its undulating surface.

**7 ▶ Apply a light tone to the flagon** The creamy paper is close to the local colour of the body of the flagon. Mix a very pale wash of Payne's grey with a touch of raw sienna and lay this over the flagon, leaving a light area on the left-hand side.

## DEVELOPING THE PICTURE

You have created a monochrome study in which the shapes and broad tonal arrangements have been mapped out. You can now start to apply areas of local colour – on the apples and pumpkins, for example. From now on, the picture will progress surprisingly quickly.

### REMOVING PAINT FOR HIGHLIGHTS

**TROUBLESHOOTER**

There are various tricks for creating lighter areas. You can lift out colour with a piece of tissue or cloth while the paint is still wet. Once the paint is dry, you can lighten it slightly by rubbing it lightly with an eraser as shown here. You can even re-wet areas with a brush, then lift out patches of colour.

**8 ◀ Start to paint the apples** Mix some cadmium yellow pale with just a touch of viridian and lay in patches of colour for the apples. Mix scarlet, permanent rose and a little raw sienna to create a warm russet tone. Apply this to the apples, following the curve of the fruit.

**◀ Add burnt umber to the wash of cadmium yellow deep and scarlet to give a warm chocolate brown for the flagon.**

**9 ▶ Add local colour to the pumpkins** Mix cadmium yellow deep with a touch of scarlet and apply a wash of this colour to the pumpkins. Lay the colour in bands that follow the ribbing of the vegetable, leaving some areas of paper or original wash for the highlights.

**10 ▲ Paint the glaze on the flagon** Mix burnt umber with the remains of the orange wash for the brown glaze on the flagon. Suggest the reflective surface with dabs of wash on the handle. Elsewhere, apply the wash more broadly, allowing it to build up in some areas of shadow. Leave tiny areas of bare paper for brilliant highlights.

## 11 ▶ Suggest the basket weave

Mix a dilute wash of burnt umber with a little raw sienna, and use the tip of the brush to 'draw' the dark lines of shadow between the woven strands of the basket. Don't put in every strand, otherwise the result will tend to look mechanical and unconvincing.

## 12 ▲ Develop the pitcher

Wash a mix of burnt sienna and permanent rose over the pitcher. Dry the painting using a hair-dryer. Add burnt umber to the wash to paint the shadow of the basket on the pitcher and to create the dark tone within the lip. Dilute the wash for the band of dark tone down the right side of the pitcher, using the brush tip to indicate some of the ridges that run around its lower half.

## 13 ◀ Add the darkest tones

Tighten up the apples with a little green and red. Mix raw umber with a little Payne's grey and, using the brush tip, add crisp details around the rim of the basket. Apply washes of dark tone between the apples to give them solidity and form. Darken the wash and paint a bold shadow on the wall behind the pumpkin.

# A FEW STEPS FURTHER

*The image is now fully resolved, the colours accurate and the forms solidly established. With watercolour, however, it is possible to continue tightening up the image, adding details and textures to achieve a more 'finished' result.*

## 14 ▶ Enhance the colour

Mix cadmium yellow deep with a touch of scarlet and raw umber and wash colour around the left side of the left-hand pumpkin. Mix raw sienna and light red and apply this over the body of the pitcher to soften the gradations of tone.

## *Express yourself*
## A simpler composition

By removing the basket of apples from the set-up, the artist has entirely changed the mood of the composition. With fewer objects and with more space in the foreground, the arrangement is simpler and more static. The artist has developed the tones to create a dramatic **chiaroscuro** reminiscent of the carefully worked paintings of the Dutch and Spanish Masters of the seventeenth century (an example of which would be *Still Life with Brass Pot* by Floris van Schooten).

**15** ▼ **Add details** Use a dilute wash of burnt umber to paint details around the stem of the pumpkin. Add light red to this wash, dilute it and lightly indicate the gaps between the tiles on the surface. Mix Payne's grey and raw sienna, and lay bands of colour to show the faceted surface of the flagon, allowing the paint to dry between each application of wash to achieve hard edges.

**16** ▲ **Add highlights** When the paper is totally dry, use a sharp knife to scratch back into the paper to create an area of highlight around the rim of the pitcher.

◄ **Cadmium yellow deep is a warm yellow that makes an ideal base colour for the pumpkins. Adding a little scarlet will give a range of orange shades.**

# THE FINISHED PICTURE

**A  Paper tone**
The warm tone of the paper shows through the watercolour paint in places and becomes part of the picture in its own right.

**B  Layers of wash**
Carefully applied layers of orange wash describe the surface appearance of the pumpkin and indicate its solid form.

**C  Highlights**
By adding a little dark tone near the highlights on the pitcher and flagon, you can make these light touches appear brighter.

# Bowl of eggs

*These eggs nestling in a bed of straw create an unusual image of quiet and simple beauty. Capture their delicate colours and tones in watercolour.*

S ometimes the simplest subjects make the most telling images. Inspired by the soft colours of these eggs, the artist arranged them in a bowl lined with straw, and painted them with subtle watercolour washes.

Watercolour is the ideal medium for a subject such as this. When the paint is applied in thin washes, light passes through to the white paper and reflects back through the colours, giving them a marvellous luminosity. It is important to mix the correct quantities of paint and water to obtain the right consistency.

The secret is to start off with the lightest of washes and gradually build colour, tone and form with a series of thin, transparent layers, rather like delicate sheets of tissue paper. By working in this way, you achieve tonal depth while retaining the freshness and sparkle of the colours.

▲ **The softly modelled forms and nuances of colour in this painting are achieved by laying wash over wash.**

## FIRST STROKES

**1 ▶ Draw with the brush** Wet the paper with clean water and a No. 8 round brush. While it dries off a little, mix a very weak wash of raw sienna and a touch of ivory black. Use this to rough in the eggs and the shadows between them, 'drawing' with a No. 6 round brush. Next, use a cooler mix of Payne's grey and raw umber to outline the bowl.

**2 ◀ Define the eggs** Give more definition to the eggs by painting the shadows around and between them with the Payne's grey/raw umber mix, adding a hint of permanent rose for the warmer shadows. 'Negative' painting in this way is easier than trying to draw the shapes of the eggs themselves. It also helps to integrate the objects in the composition because you are 'sculpting' them out of the page, rather than imposing them on to it.

## EXPERT ADVICE
### Thumbnail sketches

No matter how simple your subject, you still need to compose it well and position it effectively on the paper. Don't go for the obvious solution of placing the subject centrally. By cropping in on the bowl and placing it off-centre, you will create a more dynamic composition. Try out different ideas by observing the set-up through a viewfinder and making some small thumbnail sketches before starting to paint.

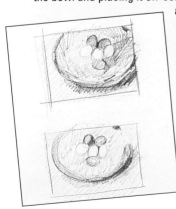

**3 ▲ Make a base wash for the straw** Mix a weak wash of cadmium yellow and a little permanent rose to make a warm underwash for the straw. Brush it on loosely, going over the brown eggs, too. Leave to dry.

**4** ▲ **Paint the darkest brown egg** Mix a rich, warm brown from Indian yellow and Indian red, and block in the darkest of the brown eggs. While this is still damp, rinse the brush and flick it dry, then lift out the soft highlight on the egg. A white highlight would look wrong here; allow some of the surrounding colour to flow back on the damp paper, so that the highlight is just a shade lighter than the egg itself.

**5** ▲ **Paint the next brown egg** Add permanent rose to the mixture and lighten it with a little more water. Paint the brown egg on the right – it is slightly cooler and paler in colour than the first one. Create a soft highlight on the top of the egg as before.

**6** ▶ **Work on the blue and green eggs**

Rinse the brush, then make up a weak mix of cerulean with a touch of Indian yellow to colour the blue egg. Paint the green egg with a mixture of cobalt blue and cadmium yellow, again thinly diluted. While this wash is still just damp, paint the shadow on the egg with a weak wash of ivory black and raw umber. Leave the painting to dry.

## DEVELOPING THE PICTURE

Now that the basic shapes and colours of the eggs are established with pale washes, introduce deeper tones to build up form and detail.

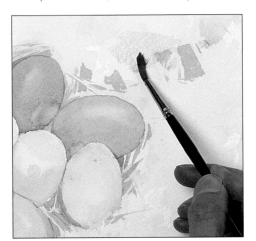

**7** ◄ **Show the shadows in the straw** In this step, you will be defining the dark shadows in the centre of the straw, while leaving the thin strands unpainted. Mix a warm shadow colour from raw sienna, Indian red and a little ivory black, and touch in the shadows with the tip of the brush, cutting around the lines of the straw.

**8** ▲ **Work on the straw** Make sure the shadows are completely dry before you start to paint the light tones of the straw itself. For this, you will need a pale mix of Indian yellow warmed with a touch of Indian red. Use long, sweeping strokes to suggest the tangled mass of straw, working loosely so that the pale underwash shows through.

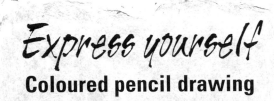

## Express yourself
## Coloured pencil drawing

Here, the artist has produced the same subject using coloured pencils instead of watercolours. In fact, coloured pencils are similar to watercolours in that the coloured pigment is semi-transparent, allowing light to reflect off the paper. The artist has used the sides, rather than the points, of the pencils to drift the colours on lightly, like watercolour washes. The pigment has caught on the tooth of the cartridge paper, producing a subtle, granular finish, which adds to the delicacy of the image. Light and shadow are created by optical mixing – using a network of overlaid strokes to produce hues and tones that interact vibrantly.

**9** ▲ **Deepen the shadows** Mix a strong wash of burnt umber and, using a No. 2 round brush, block in the darkest shadows around the eggs. Using the No. 6 round brush, define the bowl's rim with a mix of Payne's grey and burnt umber.

**10** ▲ **Strengthen the eggs** Mix burnt sienna and burnt umber to deepen the topmost egg. Add permanent rose and more water to the wash and paint the other brown egg. Mix in Payne's grey for the shadow. Lift highlights out from the damp washes. Mix cerulean and Indian yellow for the blue egg, adding a second wash for the shadow. Wash pale cadmium yellow over the green egg, with pale raw umber and black for the shadow. Add a wash of burnt sienna, permanent rose and black to the bottom egg.

**11** ▲ **Add more straw texture** Mix a base wash of Indian red and a hint of black, diluted to a mid tone. Using the No. 2 brush, suggest strands of straw with linear strokes. Define light and dark tones by adding more or less water to the wash. Where the straw is warm in colour, add cadmium yellow or permanent rose; where cool, add Payne's grey.

**12** ▲ **Adjust the tones** Use the No. 2 brush to darken the shadows around the eggs with burnt umber to give a sense of the eggs 'nestling' in a well in the straw. Indicate the direction of the light by slightly darkening the tone of the straw on the left side of the bowl with further strokes of the cool colour used in step 11.

## A FEW STEPS FURTHER

*The picture works well at this stage, with a nice textural contrast between the smooth, round eggs and the scratchy, dry straw. All that remains is to model the eggs a little more, complete the background and add some final details.*

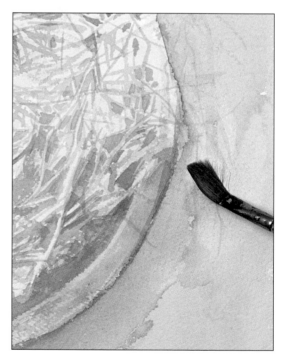

**13** ▲ **Strengthen the shadows** Strengthen the shadow on the right-hand brown egg with the No. 6 brush and a mix of Indian red, burnt sienna and a little Payne's grey and Indian yellow. Use cerulean, Indian yellow and a hint of black on the blue egg, and raw umber and black on the green egg. Mix permanent rose and black for the egg next to the green one. Remember to keep all the washes thin and transparent – they are only slightly darker than the eggs themselves.

**14** ▲ **Add a simple background wash** Mix a weak wash of permanent rose, Indian yellow and ivory black, and brush it loosely over the background with a No. 6 filbert brush. Darken it with more black, then add the cast shadow of the bowl while the underwash is still damp. Let it bleed out softly at the edges.

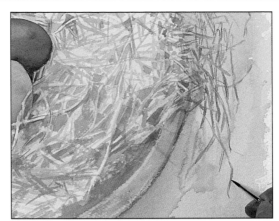

**16 ▶ Add the speckles** Define the rim of the bowl with the No. 6 brush and a wash of raw umber, burnt sienna and black. Leave to dry. Dot specks of burnt umber over the rim. Place a piece of tracing paper over the picture, trace round the lower brown egg and cut it out with a craft knife. Place the tracing paper back in position. Hold it steady while you lightly spatter the brown egg with burnt umber, using a stencil brush or old toothbrush.

**15 ▲ Finish off the straw** Mix a base wash of Indian red, Indian yellow and ivory black, and paint the strands of straw overhanging the bowl with the No. 2 brush. Vary the tones by adding burnt umber and more ivory black for the darker strands.

# THE FINISHED PICTURE

**A Transparent layers**
Layers of transparent watercolour were used to build up the smooth forms of the eggs while retaining their delicacy.

**B Mood**
Soft tones and muted shades of blue, green and brown evoke a mood of quiet tranquillity in the composition.

**C Vignetting**
The simple, subdued background fades away gradually at the edges, concentrating the viewer's attention on the bowl of eggs.

# Statue in watercolour

*When painting statues, you can benefit from the sculptor's ability to convey interesting poses, as well as using your own figure-drawing skills.*

When painting in a town or city, you don't have to record entire streets or buildings in order to create an interesting picture. Public buildings, squares and parks often have fountains, monuments and figurative sculptures in or around them, and these can make fascinating studies in their own right. If you are interested in figure painting, you will get valuable practice by drawing and painting from sculpture – with the distinct advantage that the figures never move.

In this painting, the artist has used watercolour to create a striking image of a statue of the Roman god Neptune, which stands outside the Palazzo Vecchio in Florence, Italy. Individual strokes of colour convey the strongly modelled forms of the figures, and tonal depth is built up by overlaying washes.

## Accurate drawing

When painting a sculpted figure, the underlying drawing is very important. Make this as accurate as you can without recording excessive detail. Working from direct observation produces the best results, but attempting to paint in a city street or square can be difficult, so you might have to work from sketches, notes and photographs. Early morning and late afternoon are good times to paint because the sun is low in the sky and casts strong shadows that accentuate form and volume.

▶ **Sculpted figures can be as rewarding to paint as models in a life class. The muscular form of this statue has been built up with overlaid washes of watercolour.**

## FIRST STROKES

**1 ▶ Sketch the statue** Start to draw the statue in pencil, making sure the proportions of the main figure and the two smaller ones are correct. Work lightly, feeling out the forms as you go. If you make a mistake, simply re-draw on top of it. This will convey the flowing forms of the figures better than a single outline.

**2 ▲ Start to block in the shadows** Finish drawing the statue, then very lightly sketch the roof of the background building and the outlines of the clouds. Mix a cool, mid-toned wash of raw umber with a touch of burnt sienna and start to block in the shadows on the male figure with a No. 4 round brush.

**3 ▲ Start to add some lights** Mix a pale wash of raw sienna and start to put in the light, warm tones on the figures. Skip your brush lightly over the paper, creating flowing strokes that begin to emphasize the forms of the figures.

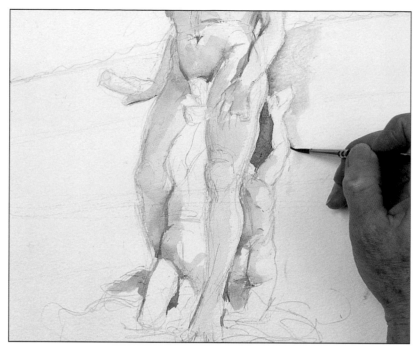

**4** ▲ **Develop the light and shadow** Continue building up the forms, using the cool wash from step 2 for the shadows and the warm wash from step 3 for the lights. Strengthen the darker shadows with further washes of the raw umber/burnt sienna mix. Start to put in a light tone of the same mix around the statue to separate it from the building behind.

**5** ▶ **Add more colour to the background** Mix a dilute wash of raw umber, warmed with a touch of crimson lake. Wash this over the background building with a No. 10 round brush.

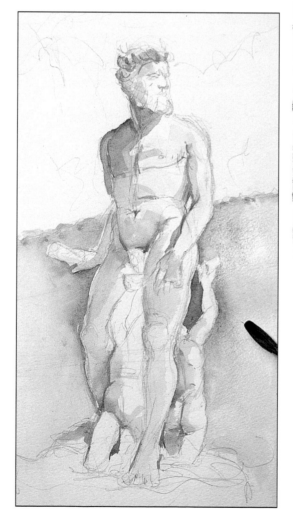

## *Express yourself*
## Working in soft pastel

Using soft pastels, you can build up layers of colour to model the forms of a figure, just as you can with watercolour. In this drawing, the dark tones on the left of the statue are achieved by applying burnt sienna and raw umber shades over the warmer golds used for the lighter side. You can achieve further modelling on the body with finely hatched lines. Create hazy, blended colours for the sky and the building by rubbing them softly with your finger or a torchon.

▶ **Washes of burnt sienna, raw umber and raw sienna (clockwise from top) are used to model the figures.**

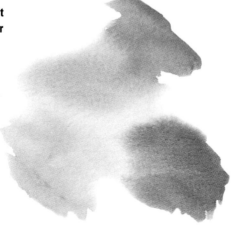

## DEVELOPING THE PICTURE

Now that the main elements of the composition have been blocked in, step back and review your progress so far. The next stage is to develop the detail and modelling of the statue using overlaid washes of transparent colour.

**6 ▲ Add mid tones** Using the No. 4 brush, emphasize the roof-line and the shadow around the statue with a darker wash of the shadow mix from step 4. Continue working over the figures and base, developing the forms with further superimposed washes. Dilute the shadow colour with more water and use this to introduce some mid tones.

**7 ▲ Introduce some warmth** Continue modelling the forms of the figures with overlaid washes, mixing raw sienna and a little French ultramarine for the grey shadows. Then mix a wash of crimson lake and use the No. 10 brush to apply this loosely over the background buildings, letting the underwash applied in step 5 show through the gaps.

### TROUBLE SHOOTER

### SCRATCHING OUT

When you are painting a small, detailed area, such as the head of the statue, it is easy to overwork with the brush, adding too much paint and losing sight of the small, white highlights that are vital in conveying the sparkle of light. To retrieve the highlights, simply allow the paint to dry, then gently scrape back to the white paper with the sharp blade of a scalpel or craft knife.

**8 ▲ Develop the details of the face** Mix a more concentrated wash of raw umber and burnt sienna and use this to define the details on the statue's face, hair and beard with a No. 2 brush. Keep in mind the main areas of light and shadow falling on the head, and paint the details lighter or darker accordingly.

**9** ▲ **Strengthen the forms** Using the No. 4 brush, continue to model the figures with warm and cool colours as before. Deepen the strongest shadows with transparent washes of French ultramarine and strengthen the warmest highlights with yellow ochre.

**10** ▶ **Paint the sky** Use the No. 10 round brush to dampen the sky area, so that you can suggest storm clouds with wet-on-wet washes. Mix French ultramarine and Prussian blue for the cool grey clouds, and add touches of crimson lake for the warmer clouds. Paint some loose strokes of the blue-grey mix on to the background buildings.

## A FEW STEPS FURTHER

*The painting is now almost complete. All that is required are the final touches of extreme light and dark that will sharpen the image and bring it into focus.*

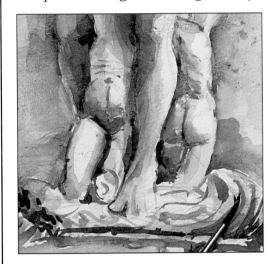

**11** ◄ **Accentuate the darks** Mix a strong dark colour from raw umber, burnt sienna and Prussian blue. Use the No. 2 brush to accentuate the figures by painting the dark shadows between them. With the same mix, define the carving on the plinth. Leave the painting to dry thoroughly.

**12** ▲ **Suggest the fountains** Hint at the splashing water of the fountains around the statue by scratching into the dry paint with the tip of a sharp blade to create a few broken lines.

## THE FINISHED PICTURE

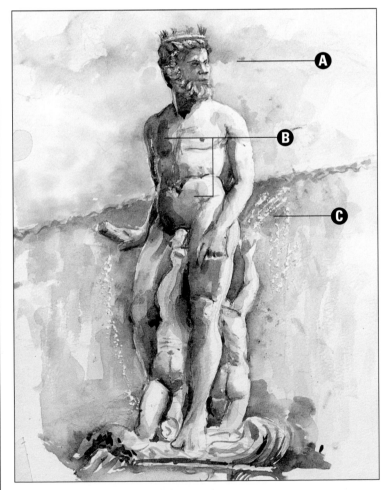

**A Dramatic licence**
To be in keeping with the imposing statue, the sky was deliberately made a little darker and more dramatic than in the original scene.

**B Warm and cool**
Overlaid strokes of warm and cool colour defined the forms of the figures.

**C Simple background**
The details of the background building were treated very loosely in order to focus attention on the statue.

# Sunflowers and bamboo leaves

*Contrasting colours and shapes give an exuberant quality*
*to this simple but striking arrangement of flowers and leaves.*

**W**atercolour has a translucency that is perfect for interpreting the delicate, filmy quality of flower petals. The secret to achieving this effect is to work in a logical progression from the first pale areas of wash to the final subtle details.

At first glance, this flower painting looks complex and highly finished. Closer inspection, however, shows that it is actually painted quite simply, but with careful attention to modulations of tone and colour.

## Building up washes

Working with watercolour washes can be tricky. If you allow the paint to dry between each wash, the colour acquires a hard outline. Applying a wash to a still-wet area, on the other hand, can produce lovely effects, but you risk losing control and creating a mess. The best method for painting flowers is to apply a second wash while the first is still just damp; in this way the colours merge softly to produce subtle effects.

## The time factor

Flowers are living things and will not stay still when placed in a vase. Blooms will open or close depending on the light, leaves may droop and petals fall – as happened during the course of this painting. The changes should not be too great, but it is important to make an accurate drawing of the group and leave it unchanged as the painting develops.

▶ **This arrangement exploits the contrast between elegant, sword-like bamboo leaves and full, rounded sunflower heads.**

## FIRST STEPS

**1** ▼ **Make an outline drawing** Using a sharp 2B pencil, draw the sunflowers and bamboo leaves in outline, but don't attempt to suggest shading or texture. Extend the image right out to the edges of the picture area.

**2** ▼ **Begin the first sunflower** Mix a wash of cadmium yellow pale, warmed with a hint of cadmium orange. Working on dry paper, start to paint the individual flower petals with a No. 3 soft round brush. Add a touch of Winsor violet to the mix for the shaded petals.

**3** ▲ **Develop the petals** Continue to paint the sunflower petals, looking for the subtle changes of tone and warmth or coolness created by light and shadow. When you have painted in all the palest petals, strengthen the wash with more cadmium orange, then put in the deeper tones and the shadows beneath and between the petals. Leave the painting to dry.

▶ The palette for the petals was based on cadmium orange and cadmium yellow pale, with cadmium scarlet and alizarin crimson added to darken some tones.

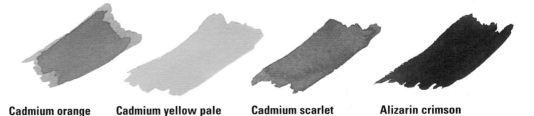

Cadmium orange    Cadmium yellow pale    Cadmium scarlet    Alizarin crimson

**4** ▼ **Paint the centre of the sunflower** Make a thin, loosely mixed wash of burnt sienna, Van Dyke brown and a touch of ultramarine violet, and fill in the flower centre. Don't overwork the paint – let it puddle in places. As the individual colours are only partially mixed, you will achieve a subtly variegated effect rather than a flat wash of colour.

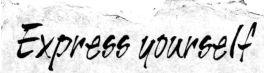

## A quick impression

Speed and spontaneity are the keynotes in this very different version of the sunflowers. A rapid pencil sketch is overlaid with equally rapid brush strokes and the fluid watercolour washes are allowed to fuse while wet. The aim is to capture the exuberant 'personality' of the flowers and leaves. Elements on the left of the arrangement are half-suggested, allowing the viewer's imagination to complete the image.

**5** ◄ **Add darker browns** When the base wash is almost dry, darken it with more ultramarine violet. Then, with the tip of the brush, make small, broken brush strokes and stippled marks to suggest the texture of the closely packed seeds.

**6** ▶ **Bring in some greens** Mix a dilute wash of sap green, enriched with a touch of cadmium orange. Use the brush tip to paint the greenish sepals surrounding the petals. Darken the wash with a hint of ultramarine to suggest the way the sepals curl over into shadow. Use the same colours to fill in the bamboo leaf. Leave to dry.

► For the leaves, sap green is warmed with cadmium lemon and cadmium yellow pale, and cooled with ultramarine.

 **Sap green**

 **Cadmium lemon**

**Cadmium yellow pale**

**Ultramarine**

**7** ▼ **Paint the second sunflower** Return to the yellow and green mixes used in steps 2, 3 and 6 to paint the petals and sepals of the next sunflower. Leave to dry. Add a little alizarin crimson or cadmium scarlet to the deepest yellow mix and go over some of the darker petals again.

**8** ▲ **Add more leaves** Fill in the flower centre as in steps 4 and 5. Then paint more bamboo leaves. Use sap green as the base colour, adding a little ultramarine and cadmium lemon for the stronger, cooler greens, as on the large vertical leaf. For warmer, yellower leaves, mix cadmium yellow pale with the sap green. For the faded leaves, add a hint of Van Dyke brown. Vary the tones of the leaves by adding more or less water to the paint. Leave to dry.

**EXPERT ADVICE
Sharp-edged leaves**

Bamboo leaves have clean, sharp edges. To capture these, fill in the leaf with colour, then, while the paint is still wet, rinse your brush and stroke a little clean water on to the centre of the leaf. The water will carry some of the pigment to the edges of the leaf, where it will dry, leaving a dark outline.

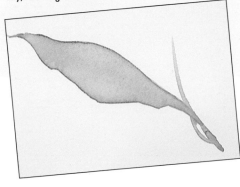

**9** ▲ **Complete the third flower** Fill in the chinks of the blue background showing between the flowers and leaves with a wash of ultramarine. Build up the petals on the third sunflower with the mixtures used in step 7, then fill in the centre with tones of brown as before. Add cast shadows to the bamboo leaves with a mix of sap green and ultramarine.

## DEVELOPING THE PICTURE

The flowers and leaves are now almost complete and it is time to work on the other elements in the composition – the vase and background. These should be more loosely painted, so as not to compete with the main subject.

**10 ◄ Work on the background**
Loosely brush a watery wash of ultramarine over the upper right of the picture to give a suggestion of background. Make the wash deeper near the flowers, fading out towards the edges of the paper.

**11 ◄ Paint the vase**
Mix sap green, cadmium lemon and cadmium orange, and paint the vase, leaving flecks of white paper for highlights. While the wash is damp, drop in a tiny bit of ultramarine at the top of the vase, allowing it to bleed.

**12**▼ **Paint the fallen petals** Cut flowers may shed some of their petals, especially on a warm day, but you can use this to your advantage. They add interest to the bottom half of the composition, often a rather 'dead' area, and they also provide a natural colour echo of the flowers themselves. Paint the petals with different shades of yellow, just as you did for the petals on the flowers.

**13**▼ **Finish the vase** Complete the leaves on the left as in step 8. For the unglazed base of the vase, mix burnt sienna and chrome yellow. Dab on Van Dyke brown and alizarin crimson for the darker tones on the left, suggesting the vase's rounded form. Let these colours bleed together wet-on-wet.

**14**▼ **Add more background wash** With a No. 5 soft round brush, fill in the background on the left-hand side of the picture with a wash of ultramarine – make it slightly stronger than the wash on the right-hand side. Brush the colour on loosely, leaving a few tiny flecks of white paper to give it some sparkle.

**15**▲ **Complete the background wash** Take the blue wash down into the foreground area and into the lower right of the picture. While this is still damp, float on a few small strokes of dilute cadmium yellow pale here and there, just to the right of the flowers and also just beneath the vase.

## A FEW STEPS FURTHER

*The yellow sunflowers are almost complete and are enhanced by the blue background. Just add some final shadows and details to give the image more depth.*

**16** ▶ **Add a cast shadow** While the blue wash is still damp (but not wet) mix ultramarine, ultramarine violet and a hint of Van Dyke brown and put in the sliver of dark shadow underneath the vase. Let the shadow edge bleed softly into the surrounding blue wash.

**17** ▲ **Create dappled light** Work over some of the leaves with very dilute ultramarine applied with crisscross strokes. This gives the effect of shadows with tiny chinks of light in between.

## THE FINISHED PICTURE

**A** Transparent washes

**B** Exciting shapes

**C** Blue background

**18** ▲ **Complete the sunflowers** Mix cadmium yellow pale, cadmium orange and alizarin crimson. Add touches of this warm yellow to the petals and dot a few highlights on the flower centres.

**A Transparent washes**
Delicate washes of watercolour allow light to reflect back off the paper and suggest the translucent petals.

**B Exciting shapes**
The bamboo leaves were extended right to the edges of the picture to create lively positive and negative shapes.

**C Blue background**
A blue background wash contrasts effectively with the bright yellow flowers while harmonizing with the greens.

# A lemon, a pear and an orange

*How do you capture the texture of fruit? Try stippling, spattering and blotting to apply the paint – and using fine sandpaper to remove it!*

Watercolour is a versatile medium and a wide range of techniques can be marshalled to build up texture. In this step-by-step, spattering, blotting and sanding down are used alongside traditional layered washes. This helps to capture the texture of three fruits and create a rich and embellished paint surface. And these interesting paint effects are combined with an understated composition to produce an unusual and striking picture.

## Emphasize the abstract

Note how, as well as accurately describing the fruits, the artist has focused on the abstract qualities of the subject. Three fruits are ranged along a shelf in such a way that the picture area is divided roughly into thirds and the spaces between, below and above the lemon, pear and orange become important elements in the composition. The fruits are set in a shallow picture space against a vibrant red backdrop that emphasizes their simple shapes.

Try setting up a similar arrangement for yourself – the finished display should look contrived rather than natural. Select fruits for their shape, colour and texture, place them on a shelf at eye level and arrange them so as to produce interesting shapes between and around them. You don't want the fruits to look as if you have just happened upon them.

Use a thick, good-quality watercolour paper and 'work' the paint surface, building up colour with layers of washes and textural effects. Add to the impact of these techniques by using gum arabic – an additive that gives the paint a more glossy finish and makes it easier to re-wet washes. (Note that it also slows the drying time.)

## Tackling the subject

Work in a controlled way in the early stages, observing the subject carefully, then laying in the first simple washes on the lemon, pear and orange. Allow early first washes to dry, then apply a second layer of colour to each.

As the individual fruit images begin to emerge, you can start to introduce the textural elements and details that differentiate them – the smoothness of the pear's skin and its subtle blush of red, and the pitted surface of the orange and lemon skins. As the painting progresses, move away from pure description and add spontaneous marks, so that the forms begin to take on a life of their own.

## YOU WILL NEED

Piece of 640gsm (300lb) NOT watercolour paper 38 x 56cm (15 x 22in)

3B graphite stick

14 watercolours: lemon yellow; cadmium yellow; sap green; cadmium red; cadmium orange; permanent mauve; Payne's grey; yellow ochre; raw umber;

permanent magenta; burnt umber; cadmium red deep; vermilion; ivory black

Brushes: Nos. 6 and 12 rounds

Gum arabic

Kitchen paper

Fine-grade sandpaper

Ruler; stiff paper or thin card

◄ Here, the bright, flat background contrasts with the textured surfaces of the fruits.

## FIRST STEPS

**1** ▼ **Lay in the underdrawing** Using a 3B graphite stick, make an outline underdrawing, putting in just enough information to plot the location of your washes. Work lightly so that the lines don't show in the final painting.

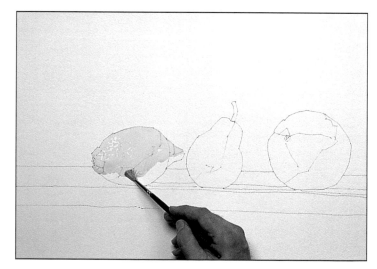

**2** ▲ **Wash in the lemon** Mix a wash of lemon yellow and cadmium yellow, then, using a No. 6 round brush, apply a wash of colour to the lemon. Stipple the paint on with the tip of the brush to create the highlights on the dimpled skin near the navel, where the fruit receives the light.

**3** ▼ **Paint the pear** Add sap green to the yellow mix and use this to define the left side of the pear. While the wash is still wet, flood in a wash of cadmium red on the right. Don't be tempted to tamper with it – allow the colour to blend into the green wash in its own way.

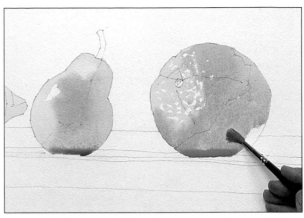

**4** ▲ **Paint the orange** Take the green wash around the rest of the pear, allowing the red blush to flood into it. Mix a wash of cadmium orange and cadmium yellow and apply to the orange, stippling where its surface catches the light.

## DEVELOPING THE PICTURE

Develop the fruits by laying a series of washes, allowing the paint to dry between applications. These overlapping transparent and semi-transparent washes give the watercolour its depth and luminosity.

**5** ▼ **Add texture to the lemon** Check that the first wash on the lemon is thoroughly dry. Then, using a mix of cadmium yellow with a little cadmium orange, stipple colour on to the light part of the fruit. Take a flat wash over the rest of the lemon.

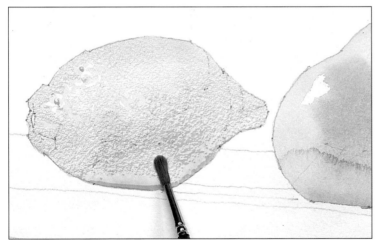

**6** ▲ **Develop tone on the pear** Apply a sap green wash to the pear, then flood in cadmium red, allowing the colours to bleed together as in step 3. Add a touch of permanent mauve to the green wash to make a dark tone and take this around the right-hand side and base of the pear, which are turned away from the light.

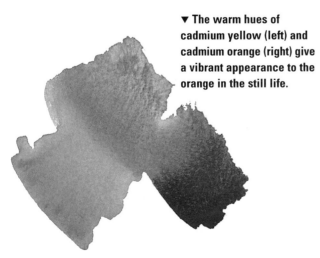

▼ **The warm hues of cadmium yellow (left) and cadmium orange (right) give a vibrant appearance to the orange in the still life.**

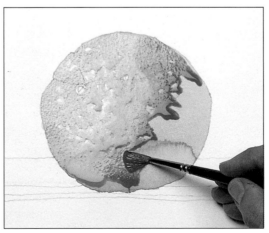

**7** ◄ **Intensify the orange** Mix a wash of cadmium orange, then use a stippling technique on the lit surface of the fruit, as in step 4. Take the rich colour over the rest of the fruit.

**8** ▼ **Apply a third layer** Add cadmium orange to the yellow mix from step 5 and stipple over the left and centre of the lemon. Darken the mix with permanent mauve and Payne's grey, and paint the shaded part of the fruit.

**9** ▲ **Add dark tones** Mix permanent mauve and Payne's grey into the sap green wash to darken the shadow on the pear. Add cadmium red to the mix and flood into the red blush, spattering droplets for texture. Paint the stalk with dilute Payne's grey. Moving to the orange, use cadmium orange to paint furrows and stipple around the navel. Add permanent mauve, Payne's grey and gum arabic to the orange wash for the shadow.

## Express yourself
### Close-up pumpkin

Here, the focus is on the tough, ribbed surface of a pumpkin. Cropping in tightly removes it from its context, confusing the sense of scale and emphasizing shape, colour and texture.

**10** ▲ **Spatter with water** When the orange is dry, spatter the surface with clean water. Leave the water for a few seconds to dissolve the previous wash, then gently blot the surface with kitchen paper to create random speckles of light tone that suggest the texture of the orange peel.

▼ Washes of sap green (left) and cadmium red (right) are blended wet-on-wet to create subtly graduated colour on the pear.

**11** ▼ **Develop the dark tones** Use a yellow ochre and cadmium yellow mix for the ridges around the lemon's navel. Add Payne's grey and permanent mauve to the mix and darken the shadows. Develop the pear with further green and red washes, adding Payne's grey for the shadows and stalk. Using cadmium orange, add details to the top of the orange and flick droplets of colour on to the surface. Darken the mix with permanent mauve and Payne's grey, and apply these to the shaded areas.

**EXPERT ADVICE**
**Sandpaper highlights**

Once the watercolour washes are thoroughly dry, you can rub down the surface of the paint with a fine-grade sandpaper to create areas of highlight on the fruits. Tear off a piece of sandpaper, lay it on the surface of the dry wash, and rub gently until you get back to the paper, checking the effect as you work.

**12** ▶ **Rub down the fruits** Using the technique described in Expert Advice, rub the surfaces of the fruits with fine-grade sandpaper to create highlights. On the lemon and the pear, make smooth, white patches; on the orange, rub the surface much more gently to give a stippled effect. Spatter droplets of the colour mixes from step 11 on to the three fruits.

**13** ◀ **Lift colour** You can lift areas of colour by wetting the wash and working over the surface very gently with a brush – the effect is more subtle than that achieved with sandpaper. To do this on the orange, wet areas on the right and the bottom and work over them with the No. 6 brush to lift the colour. Rinse the brush in clean water and repeat to increase the effect.

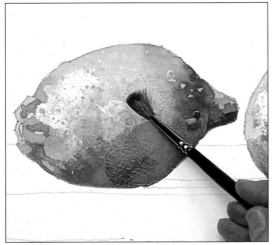

**14** ▲ **Soften colour on the lemon** Work a moist brush over the surface of the lemon at centre right to re-wet the dry wash. Lift colour as in step 13. Varying the tone in this way helps to build up the rounded form of the fruit.

**15** ◄ **Paint the shelf** Mix a wash of raw umber and cadmium orange to make a brown for the shelf. To achieve a straight edge, use a ruler as a guide – place it parallel to the shelf and lift one side away from the surface, then draw a line by resting the No. 6 brush against the raised edge and pulling it along the length of the ruler.

**16** ▲ **Add shadows** Use a dark version of the same raw umber/cadmium orange mix to paint horizontal bands of colour that suggest the grain of the wood. Mix permanent magenta, burnt umber and cadmium red, and use this dark mix for the long, horizontal shadows cast by the fruits.

**17** ▼ **Paint the shelf edge** Dilute the dark mix from step 16 and paint the shadow along the edge of the shelf. This establishes a frontal plane and creates a sense of recession.

**18** ▶ **Paint a bright background** Mix a large quantity of cadmium red deep and vermilion. Use a No. 12 round brush to apply a flat wash of this colour over the background. Take the colour carefully around the edges of the fruits to refine their silhouettes. Work quickly, keeping the wet edge moving to avoid hard edges.

**19** ▶ **Add shadow under the shelf** Mix ivory black, burnt umber and Payne's grey, and use this intense dark mix for the deep shadow under the shelf. Apply the wash with the No. 12 brush.

**20** ▶ **Complete the shadow area** Take the dark mix from step 19 over the entire shadow area. Work backwards and forwards to avoid hard edges.

## A FEW STEPS FURTHER

*On re-evaluating the painting, you might feel that the shelf could benefit from more work to enhance the texture of the wood grain. Also, the shadow under the shelf could be darker, so as to match the depth and richness of colour in the red background.*

**22** ▲ **Add more texture** Use a graphite stick to draw roughly parallel lines on the surface of the shelf. This suggests more wood grain and adds linear interest.

**23** ◄ **Strengthen the shadow** Make a stronger mix of the ivory black/burnt umber/Payne's grey shadow colour. Using the No. 12 brush, apply it over the first shadow wash to make a really deep tone.

**21** ▲ **Add texture to the shelf** Cut a strip of stiff paper or thin card, and apply the dark mix from step 19 along one edge. Touch the strip on to the shelf edge to create a line of paint. Repeat the process to suggest the grain of the wood.

## THE FINISHED PICTURE

**A Dramatic background**
A bold background in a flat wash of vibrant scarlet emphasizes the shallow picture space.

**B Overlapping washes**
A network of layered washes describes the smoothly curving surface of the pear.

**C Sandpaper highlights**
The surface of the orange was rubbed down with fine sandpaper to suggest the dimpled peel.

**D Spatters and speckles**
Spattered colour and spattered and blotted drops of water build up a rich, speckled surface.

# Orange lilies

*Use two watercolours to help capture the exotic blooms and glossy leaves of these fabulous, showy flowers.*

Watercolourists love painting flowers because the medium lends itself so well to the subject matter. Watercolour possesses a sensitivity and translucency that perfectly matches the delicacy of petals.

To get the best results when tackling flower studies, spend time on your initial sketch; if necessary, make colour notes or take a digital or polaroid photo. Flowers tend to wilt – particularly under strong lights – so work quickly, as your arrangement could look quite different a couple of hours into your painting.

## Mixing or layering

When using watercolours, there are essentially two ways of blending colours – physically or optically. To mix them physically means combining two or more colours on the palette – mixing red and yellow to make orange, for example. The other method involves laying one colour over another dry one on the paper in transparent veils. For instance, if you paint yellow over red, the eye will 'read' this as orange. The artist in this project has primarily used this optical method, as it preserves the purity of the colours. Be careful not to overdo it – three layers is generally considered the maximum you can apply without muddying the colours.

In addition, to paint the lilies the artist has relied heavily on the use of

▲ **These lilies are painted with a light touch that emphasizes their fresh beauty.**

complementary colours such as orange-reds and blue-greens. These are colours that lie opposite each other on the colour wheel and so set each other off to best advantage.

## FIRST STEPS

**1 ▼ Make an initial sketch** The starting point for the painting is to make an accurate drawing. Use a 2B pencil to map the outline of the vase and the spray of lilies. Notice how the pointed leaves overlap one another.

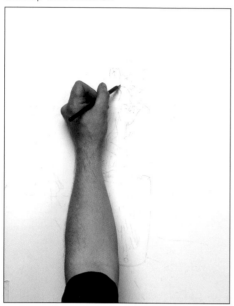

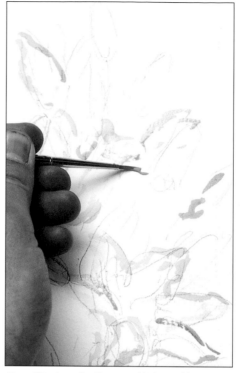

**2 ▲ Start on the flowers** Using a No. 2 round brush, lay in the outlines of the flower-heads in cadmium orange.

**3 ▶ Create hazy shadows** Make two very watery mixes of cerulean blue and raw umber. Using a 25mm (1in) flat brush, mark in some of the creases in the fabric backdrop with cerulean blue. The way the flowers are lit creates a soft shadow behind them. Wet the left side of the paper with clean water and wash in the cast shadow, using cerulean blue, then, along the left edge, raw umber.

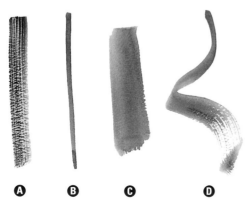

◄ **Leaf and stem shapes were made by manipulating a 25mm (1in) flat brush. Practise the following strokes before tackling the painting:**
Ⓐ **Dry brush stroke, using the flat of the brush (step 15).**
Ⓑ **Wet brush stroke, using the edge of the bristles (step 4).**
Ⓒ **Wet brush stroke, using the flat of the brush (step 8).**
Ⓓ **Flourish, using first the edge and then the width of the brush (step 5).**

Ⓐ       Ⓑ       Ⓒ       Ⓓ

**4 ▲ Draw the first leaves** Block in some of the flower petals with cadmium orange and yellow ochre, then change to a No. 2 rigger brush to start on the foliage. Draw in the stems and outline the leaves with differing strengths of Hooker's green.

## DEVELOPING THE PICTURE

Continue building up the leaves and petals with descriptive brush marks. Create form and shadow by applying layers of darker paint wet-on-dry.

**5** ▲ **Block in the leaves** Switch back to the 25mm (1in) flat brush and, with a watery olive-green wash, start shaping the leaves. Manipulate your brush to use both the broad and the narrow edge of the hairs to create the tapering shapes.

**6** ▲ **Create the illusion of glass** Watercolour is the perfect medium for suggesting glass, which combines the qualities of solidity and transparency. Mix a very dilute grey – mainly water with just a hint of ivory black – and apply this down the right-hand edge of the vase with a No. 12 flat brush.

◄ **The artist's palette shows how he avoided unnecessary mixing. The blue, greens and yellows, in particular, have been diluted, then used purely.**

## *Express yourself*
## Flower miniature

This version of the lilies is on a much smaller scale than the main project, measuring only 15 x 11cm (6 x 4½in). Worked in opaque acrylics rather than translucent watercolours, its luminous appearance and delicate texture is achieved by building up shapes and surfaces with patches and dots of colour – a technique known as 'pointillism'. Look, in particular, at the cast shadow – it is brought to life with dabs of blues and purples.

**7 ▲ Add form to the vase** Paint the base of the vase as an oval, following your initial pencil sketch. Now, switching to the No. 2 round brush, define the left-hand edge of the vase in the same watery grey.

**8 ▲ Block in some lighter leaves** With the 25mm (1in) flat brush, block in some of the broader leaves in olive green. Use your sketch as a guide, but don't feel you have to follow it slavishly.

**9 ▲ Describe the tangle of leaves** Within the vase, the leaves fight against the confines of the glass. Allowed their freedom, they spread out in every direction. Working above and below the waterline, build up the tangle of leaves, using the olive green wash from step 5 and a No. 4 round. Add cerulean blue to the olive green for darker areas.

**10 ▲ Enliven the orange** Add a touch of burnt sienna to cadmium orange to make a dark tone for the petals in shadow. Using the No. 12 flat, paint single strokes that follow the curve of the petals.

**11** ◄ **Paint the veins** If you look closely at the reference photograph, you can just make out some darker ridges on the petals. Paint these with the No. 2 round and a touch of purple.

**12** ▲ **Create two-toned buds** Use the No. 4 round and dilute Hooker's green to shape the buds. Make a stronger mix to define the darks and add cerulean blue to it to create some greenish-blue areas.

**13** ▲ **Return to the stems** Add touches of burnt sienna along the flower stems to suggest the shadows on them.

**14** ▼ **Emphasize the background** If the painting seems a little flat, you could emphasize the folds in the background fabric. Use the No. 4 round brush and a watery cerulean blue to accentuate them.

**15** ▼ **Adjust the colours** Add a few more leaves in places, using olive green. Edge the petals in cadmium red and add stamens in purple (see Expert Advice). Paint dilute cerulean blue over some leaves and apply a stronger mix along the vase rim. Darken the cast shadow with a cerulean blue/raw umber mix.

## EXPERT ADVICE
### Well-defined stamens

To make sure that the prominent, dark-coloured flower stamens really stand out, use a strong mix of purple and check that the paper is completely dry before you paint them. If there is any moisture in the paper, the paint will spread and the stamens will lose definition.

## A FEW STEPS FURTHER

*A common painting error is overworking a picture – that is, not knowing when to stop. So when you've got all the elements in place and adjusted the colours so that the balance seems right, put your brushes down. Wait until the next day before looking at it again. You never know, your picture might be perfect just as it is.*

**16** ▲ **Make the colours zing** Beef up the picture by adding strokes of strong colour among the flower-heads – use the No. 12 flat and mixes of cadmium red and cadmium orange, as well as some of the blue-greens used previously.

**17**▲ **Pick out certain flower-heads** Having applied bold strokes of colour with a flat brush, move on to the No. 4 round brush to paint stronger outlines around the petals with cadmium red and purple.

**18**▲ **Add highlights** Use permanent white gouache and the 25mm (1in) flat brush to paint a highlight on the top left of the glass vase. For a warm, radiant effect, apply cadmium yellow highlights on to and among the leaves.

## THE FINISHED PICTURE

**A Purple outlines**
The petal outlines are much more pronounced than they are in reality and make the flowers really stand out.

**B Blue shadows**
The sense of the vase's volume and mass is heightened by the strong shadow cast on to the background.

**C Line of body colour**
A fine line of permanent white gouache was added within the vase at the end of the project to suggest the water level.

# Watercolour crab

*Extend your range of watercolour techniques in responding to the challenge presented by the subtle colours and textures of a crab.*

We tend to think of a still life as being a group of objects, but a single item, when painted in an interesting way, can have just as much impact as a table groaning with fruit and vegetables. The complex forms and unusual textures in this crab provide a means of challenging your watercolour skills to the full. Don't feel inhibited – the idea is not to reproduce the crab in photographic detail, but to express the essential qualities of its appearance.

## Go with the flow

Watercolour is ideal for a spontaneous approach because it is so fluid and responsive. All sorts of textures and effects can be suggested, once you have found out how pigment and water behave.

Beginners are often afraid of watercolour because they think it is difficult to control. As this project shows, however, the best results are achieved by not controlling the paint too much; often you will find that it does much of the work for you! To paint the crab, wet the paper with clean water; work quickly and loosely, moving the brush in different directions to create a broken wash that is wetter in some parts than others – you don't want an even coating.

When the colours are applied they will flow with the water and dry unevenly, creating mottled patterns that mimic the crab's shell. By blotting with kitchen paper and adding further washes, you can build up complex patterns that would be difficult to achieve by more conventional means.

▼ Look out for interesting and unusual objects for indoor painting, and be adventurous in using watercolour techniques to depict them.

## FIRST STROKES

**1** ▶ **Draw the outline** Make a careful outline drawing of the crab using a sharp HB pencil. Don't attempt any shading, but outline the highlighted areas on the shell, some of which will be masked out.

**YOU WILL NEED**

Sheet of 400gsm+ (140lb+) NOT watercolour paper

HB pencil

Small, old watercolour brush for applying masking fluid

Tinted masking fluid

Brushes: Nos. 11, 6 and 2 round

Jar of water

6 watercolours: raw sienna; burnt sienna; cadmium orange; cadmium red; burnt umber; French ultramarine

Kitchen paper

Mixing palette or dish

**2** ▼ **Mask out the highlights** Use a very small, old paint brush to apply masking fluid to the small highlights you have outlined on the shell of the crab. Leave to dry.

**3** ▲ **Apply the underwash** Before applying any colour, load a No. 11 round brush with clean water and work it over the shape of the crab with fast, random strokes so that some areas are wetter than others. Don't worry if the water goes over the pencil lines – it will add to the unforced effect you are aiming for. Now dip the brush into some undiluted raw sienna and apply it randomly. The paint will flow with the water and create strong tones and lighter ones as it mixes with either damp or dryer areas.

## TROUBLE SHOOTER

### REMOVING HARD EDGES

If the underwash dries before you have a chance to apply a second wash over it, the second wash will dry with an unwanted hard edge. To avoid this, simply drop some water from the tip of the brush on to the edge where the two colours meet and gently work them together.

**4** ▶ **Blot with kitchen paper** While the surface is still wet, blot some of the highlight areas on the main body of the crab with crumpled kitchen paper, using a press-and-lift motion. This forces the paint into the fibres of the paper, increasing the textural effects on the crab's shell.

## DEVELOPING THE PICTURE

Having completed the underwash, the next stage is to develop the texture and form of the crab using wet-into-wet washes. The idea is to observe your subject carefully, then allow the paint to interpret what you see.

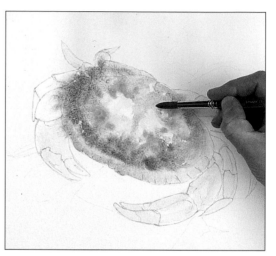

**5** ▲ **Apply burnt sienna** Working quickly before the underwash dries, apply undiluted burnt sienna around the edge of the crab's body. Just touch the tip of the brush to the paper and let the colour flow on the damp surface.

**6** ▲ **Start to build up form** Continue darkening the body with burnt sienna, except for the top and 'pie-crust' edge of the shell, which pick up more light. Touch in some cadmium orange on the top of the shell. The rounded form of the crab is beginning to emerge: the top is pale, darkening as the shell curves away from the light.

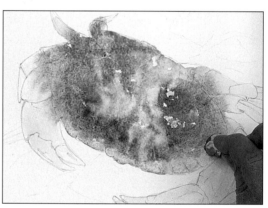

**7** ▲ **Add more colours** Carry on building up layers of paint. To suggest the blotched patterning, drip some clean water off the brush to form small pools, then touch in a little undiluted cadmium red, then some burnt sienna. Let the colours bleed into the surrounding wash.

**8** ▲ **Work on the edge of the shell** Using a wad of kitchen paper, blot the outer edge of the shell to lift out some of the paint, creating soft highlights that suggest the raised 'pie-crust' ridges. Leave the painting to dry naturally so that the water and paint settle at their own pace; using a hair-dryer will even out the marks.

**9 ◄ Add definition**
Now drop some more water from the brush on to the shell. Use the tip of a No. 6 brush to 'draw' a line of raw sienna where the rounded body meets the flat edge of the crab, adding more definition to the shape.

## EXPERT ADVICE
## White highlights

Watercolour paintings have a unique freshness that owes much to the white of the paper shining through the overlaid colours. Don't forget, you can also think of the white paper as being another 'colour'. By leaving tiny slivers and flecks of paper untouched, you can create sparkling highlights that suggest shiny surfaces. These white areas also allow the painting to 'breathe', and make the whole picture dance with light.

**10 ► Paint the darker markings**
Mix burnt umber with a touch of raw sienna and start to paint the darker markings using a No. 2 brush. Make small, fast strokes, skipping the brush over the surface to create a mottled pattern.

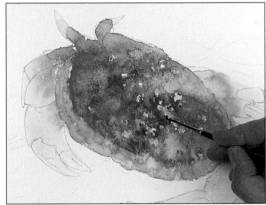

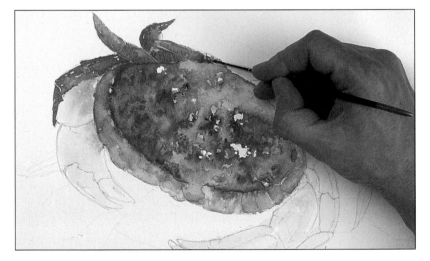

**11 ◄ Start painting the feelers** Allow the painting to dry completely, then remove the patches of masking fluid by rubbing with your finger to reveal the small, bright highlights on the shell. Now paint the first set of feelers using a slightly diluted wash of burnt sienna applied with the No. 2 brush. Don't fill in the shapes completely, but use small, broken strokes instead, allowing tiny patches of the pale underwash to show through and provide highlights. Allow to dry; because you are now working on dry paper, the paint will dry with a crisp, hard edge.

**▼ When the paint is dry you can see the interesting textural effects achieved by dropping water and wet pigment into a wet underwash, creating 'cauliflower' blooms that suggest the mottled and uneven surface of the crab's shell.**

**12 ► Add shadows**
Apply a dilute wash of burnt sienna over the feelers. Just before this dries, paint the shadows on the edges of the feelers and between the joints with a mixture of burnt umber and ultramarine. The edges will blend softly into the damp burnt sienna wash.

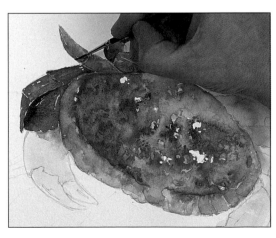

**13 ◄ Paint the claws**
Repeat steps 11 and 12 to paint the first set of claws, this time making the shadows slightly stronger. Darken the mixture with more ultramarine to paint the tips of the claws. As before, use small, broken strokes and allow slivers of the underwash to provide the highlights and reflections.

**14 ▼ Complete the claws and feelers**
Now paint the second set of claws and feelers, using the same method as for the first set. Leave the painting to dry.

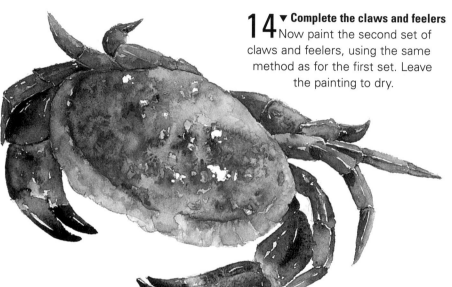

## Express yourself
### Loosen up

In this version of the same subject, the artist has worked even more loosely than before. He has also used more water: notice how some of the claws and feelers are partially dissolved, giving them an interesting 'lost-and-found' quality.

As well as painting a shadow under the crab, the artist has also suggested a white plate. This is understated so as not to detract attention from the crab, but serves to place it in context.

## A FEW STEPS FURTHER

*You might decide here that your study is complete. Sometimes adding more detail merely results in an overworked picture. But perhaps you feel your picture needs more contrast; you might also wish to add some background shadow to anchor the crab in space.*

**15 ► Strengthen texture and detail** On the body of the crab, use burnt sienna and the No. 6 brush to work up the shell and emphasize form and texture. Again, use small, quick strokes to strengthen the marks already created, particularly round the edges of the shell.

**16** ▲ **Add more darks** With the No. 2 brush go over some of the shadows on the claws and feelers with a mixture of burnt sienna and ultramarine to make them stand out. Then paint a thin, broken line along the lower edge of the crab to give it more definition. Leave to dry.

**17** ▲ **Paint the background shadow** Finally, add shadow beneath the crab for a three-dimensional effect. With the No. 6 brush, paint the shadow in raw sienna, overlaid with a pale mix of burnt sienna and ultramarine. Then rinse the brush and drip a little water on to the shadow area; the colour will dissolve into the water and dry with a soft edge.

# THE FINISHED PICTURE

**A  Rounded forms**
The rounded forms of the claws and feelers were suggested with overlaid washes, working from dark to light and leaving the brightest highlights unpainted.

**B  Mottled patterns**
The blotched patterning on the crab's shell was captured perfectly by working wet-into-wet, blotting with kitchen paper and allowing the paint to flow and dry at different rates.

**C  Softly graded shadow**
A touch of shadow helped to anchor the crab in space. The shadow is darkest directly beneath the crab, gradually fading out to nothing. This effect was achieved with a graduated wash.

# Still life of peppers

*Red and green peppers create a visually striking image that is ideally suited to watercolour washes and water-soluble pencils.*

One way of creating a sense of depth in a still life is to work over a watercolour wash. To achieve the highly effective drawing of these peppers, for example, the artist first painted thin washes of red and green watercolour over the initial sketch to give a coloured surface on which to continue the drawing with water-soluble pencils.

## Practical points

As you are using water with the paints and the coloured pencils, you will need to work on sturdy watercolour paper.

Blocks of watercolour paper are useful for this kind of exercise, where you are not intending to wet the paper very much. You can paint directly on to the top sheet, which is still secured to the block, thus avoiding having to stretch the paper first.

When you lay down the washes, change your water frequently in order to keep the paint as clean as possible. If your wash spreads too far outside the lines of the sketch, you can easily mop it up with a piece of kitchen paper. Remember, though, that as a large part

of the wash will eventually be covered by coloured pencil, you do not need to be too accurate.

## Using water-soluble pencils

Water-soluble pencils are ideal to use in conjunction with watercolours, as they can be handled like ordinary coloured pencils, but can also be dampened with a wet brush to blend and intensify their colours. You can build up the shapes of the peppers with shading, leaving the underlayer of paint showing where you want the tones to be light.

◄ The peppers are built up layer by layer, starting with an underwash of watercolour and progressing to water-soluble pencils, which are themselves wetted selectively to show form and tone.

## FIRST STROKES

**1** ▼ **Draw the outlines** Using a 4B pencil, draw the outlines of the peppers with loose strokes. Try not to make the pencil marks too strong, as you don't want them to show through the watercolour in the final picture. On the cut pepper, indicate the shape of the seed area and the pith.

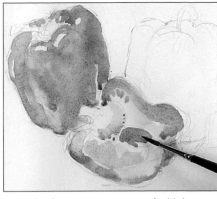

**2** ▲ **Apply a wet-on-wet wash** Using a No. 5 brush, first wash clear water over the parts of the peppers that you are going to paint. Avoid wetting the paper where the highlights will be, as you want to leave these white. Make a thin wash of alizarin crimson with a little cadmium red and paint over the wetted parts of the red peppers. Mix a little Payne's grey into the wash for the darker areas, and some sap green for the brown hollow in the cut pepper.

**3** ▶ **Begin the green pepper** Wet the green pepper again if the paper has dried out, as you need to apply the washes wet-on-wet. Leave the highlights dry, as before. Make a thin sap green wash and add a little of the previous red wash to make an olive-green colour. Paint the left side of the green pepper, then deepen the wash with more of the previous red to paint the right-hand side and the shaded part of the stalk.

**4** ▶ **Wash over the shadows** Wet the shadow areas on the right of the green pepper and under the red peppers with clear water. Avoid the edges of the previous washes so that the colours won't run together. Then brush on a dilute wash of neutral tint, mixed from all the colours on the palette, to show the grey shadows.

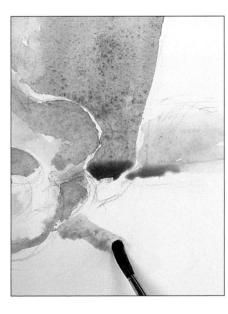

**5** ▶ **Add a few details** Leave the paint to dry. Change to a No. 3 brush to add some detail. Paint the stalks on the red peppers with sap green. Then add sap green to the original red wash to make brown. Darken the hollow in the cut pepper, dab on more seeds and paint the stalk on the green pepper. Emphasize the edges and centre of the cut pepper with a strong mix of alizarin crimson and cadmium red.

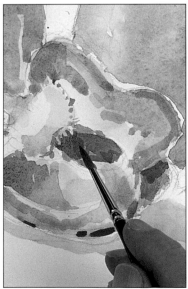

## DEVELOPING THE PICTURE

Now that the main shapes and tones of the peppers have been indicated with washes of watercolour, you can begin to define their forms more clearly with water-soluble pencils. Make sure the washes are dry before you begin – you can use a hair-dryer to speed up the process if you wish.

**6 ▲ Shade the red and green peppers** Using a rose carmine water-soluble pencil, shade over the wash on the red pepper with hatching marks until most of it is covered. Leave the highlights and some bands of lighter tone to create the pepper's ridges and curves. Change to a moss green water-soluble pencil to begin shading the green pepper. In the same way as for the red pepper, leave the pale wash showing where the tone is lighter.

**7 ▲ Work on the cut pepper** Complete the shading on the green pepper, then shade the stalks with the moss green pencil. Darken the top corner of the cut pepper with a patch of rose carmine. Using a dark orange water-soluble pencil, colour across the lighter areas of the flesh and pith of this pepper with free strokes.

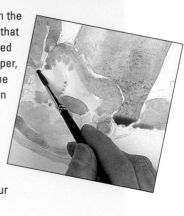

**TROUBLE SHOOTER**

### SMOOTHING OUT PUDDLES

As you are laying down the washes, you might notice that an earlier wash has gathered in a small puddle on the paper, forming a dark patch like the one at the base of the green pepper shown here.

To remove this, tip your drawing board up so that the paint runs back into the main part of the wash. In this way, the colour will be evened out.

**8 ▲ Darken the shadows** Warm up the shaded side of the red pepper with hatched lines made with an Indian red pencil. Use a medium grey pencil to deepen the colours of the cast shadows, keeping within their outlines.

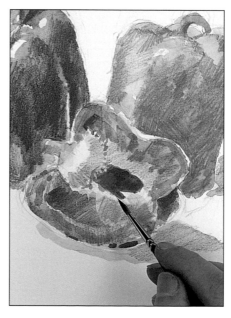

**9 ◄ Begin to wash over the pencil marks** Deepen the colour in the hollow of the cut pepper with the Indian red and dark orange pencils. Then, using the No. 3 brush, wet this area to diffuse the colour.

**10** ▼ **Add more lines and wash** Continue diffusing the colours of the pencils by washing clear water over the darker areas of the green pepper. Liven up the red pepper with the dark orange pencil, and again add a wash over these areas to intensify their colour. Add hard lines to the curves of the red pepper with the Indian red pencil, then soften them slightly with water.

## A FEW STEPS FURTHER

*The picture is now a pleasing combination of watercolour washes and pencil shading softened with added water. With additional colour, you can enhance the tones and make the peppers even more realistic.*

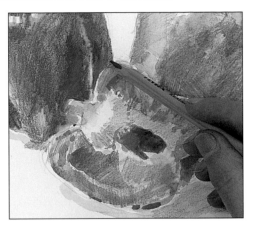

**11** ▶ **Add depth to the darkest areas** Using the medium grey pencil, deepen the darkest tones on the red pepper with just a little colour. The darker colour helps to throw the lighter colours forward in the picture.

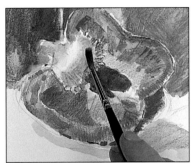

**12** ◀ **Give the picture a final wash of water** Colour in the seed area and the tops of the stalks with ochre pencil. Outline some of the seeds with the Indian red pencil, and put in some lines of texture on the edge of the cut pepper. With the rose carmine pencil, deepen the outer edge of the cut pepper. Smooth out the colours once more with the No. 3 brush.

## THE FINISHED PICTURE

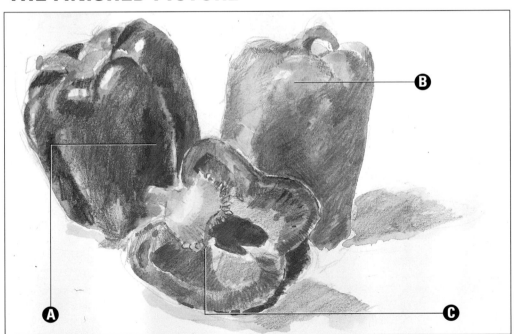

**A Dark tones**
Deeper tones were created with water-soluble pencil marks, which were then washed over to intensify the colour.

**B Light tones**
The initial pale watercolour wash shows through in places to form the light tones in the picture.

**C Sharp details**
The seeds in the cut pepper were drawn over the underlying washes with a well-sharpened water-soluble pencil.

# Shiny copper and glass

*Combine wet-on-wet and layered washes to render the reflective surface of a copper pot and the translucency of a bottle of olive oil.*

This luscious set-up with its warm colours and shiny reflective surfaces is in the great tradition of still-life painting. In the past, still lifes were usually rendered in oils, but here watercolour has been used with panache.

## Arranging a still life

A major advantage of painting a still life is the degree of control you have over the subject. When selecting objects to arrange, look for features that echo each other – in this painting, the curves and colours of the brown onions repeat those of the copper cooking pot. Too many resemblances can be boring, however, so the vertical shapes of the oil and vinegar bottles and the diagonals of the ladle and the aubergine were introduced.

## Looking at reflective surfaces

Reflective surfaces such as glass and metal provide all kinds of interesting effects. Clear glass takes its colour from the liquid within, as well as the colours seen through it and others reflected in it. With shiny metals such as copper, the local colour is modified by the reflections in its surface.

The trick with reflective surfaces is to paint exactly what you see. Try to envisage the subject as an abstract pattern of shapes, colours and tones. Remember that reflections are less precise and more muted than the objects themselves. In this set-up the reflections are so distorted by the shapes of the pot and bottles that the objects reflected are barely recognizable.

▶ **The rich colours in this still life are reflected in the various shiny surfaces, producing a warm and harmonious picture.**

Piece of 300gsm (140lb) NOT watercolour paper 40 x 56cm (16 x 22in)

HB pencil

9 watercolours: alizarin crimson; Venetian red; gold ochre; cobalt blue; lemon yellow; raw umber; yellow ochre; indigo; Winsor blue

Brushes: Nos. 12 and 14 rounds; No. 6 Chinese

Mixing palette or dish

White candle

White oil pastel

## FIRST STEPS

**1** ▲ **Sketch the set-up** Using an HB pencil, sketch the subject. Start with the sweep of the background fabric and the bigger shapes in the composition – the copper pot and the bottle of oil. Work lightly, looking for the shapes and the spaces between them. At this stage it doesn't matter if you use several tentative lines to describe a single outline – as the drawing progresses, you will decide which line is most accurate.

**2** ▲ **Block in the background colour** Mix a large wash of alizarin crimson, Venetian red and gold ochre and, using a No. 12 round brush, apply this over the red cloth. Create variations of tone by alternately adding more alizarin crimson and Venetian red to the wash. Mix cobalt blue and alizarin crimson for the shadows, and touch these in while the first wash is still wet.

◀ The rich, coppery tones of the pots and bottles are mixed from varying amounts of alizarin crimson (left), gold ochre and Venetian red.

**3 ▼ Add the coppery tones** Mix gold ochre and alizarin crimson, and use a thin wash of this mix to underpaint the onion and the sides of the copper pot. Add more gold ochre to the mix and start to touch in the dried chillies.

**4 ▼ Add candle wax** Block in the red onions with wet-on-wet washes of alizarin crimson with cobalt blue, leaving white paper for highlights. Next, reserve the highlights on the shoulders and neck of the bottles by rubbing candle wax lightly over the surface of the paper.

**5 ▼ Paint the oil bottle** Mix a gold-coloured wash from lemon yellow, raw umber and yellow ochre. Using a No. 6 Chinese brush, apply the mix to the oil bottle. Add touches of unmixed raw umber and Venetian red wet-on-wet and allow the paint to blend to capture the gradations of colour and tone in the bottle. Leave to dry.

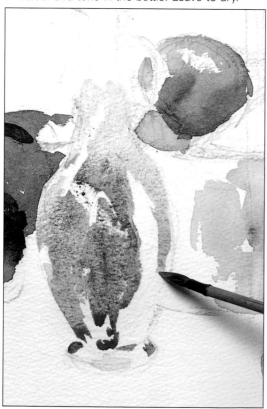

**EXPERT ADVICE**
**Test your mixes**

For a painting where subtle variations of colour and tone are required, work with a large palette and keep a test sheet of watercolour paper to hand so that you can check your mixes as you progress.

**6** ◄ **Add darker tones**
Apply touches of a raw umber/yellow ochre mix to the surface of the copper pot where the bottle is reflected in it. Then develop the bottle itself. Use raw umber for the darkest tones, flooding in Venetian red on the right.

## DEVELOPING THE PICTURE

Now begin working up the copper pot and its contents, which are the main focus of the picture. As you develop the image further, repeat colour mixes across the picture to give it harmony and visual unity.

**7** ▲ **Darken the pot** Paint the top of the oil bottle in raw umber and the gold mix from step 5. Use a cobalt blue/lemon yellow mix for the aubergine stem. Apply a dilute wash of alizarin crimson and cobalt blue to the vinegar bottle. Mix indigo, alizarin crimson and raw umber for the grey inside the pot.

**8** ▲ **Develop the pot** Paint the alizarin crimson and cobalt blue wash over the aubergine. Add more alizarin crimson and wash over the copper pot and the garlic. Leave to dry. Develop the surface of the pot with the grey mix from step 7 and strong and weak washes of Venetian red. Use a mix of alizarin crimson, gold ochre and cobalt blue for the warm brown reflections of the chillies.

**9** ▲ **Paint the chillies** Use an indigo/alizarin crimson mix for the vinegar bottle. Leave to dry, then apply a stronger mix to establish the shadows. Paint the chillies with a mix of alizarin crimson, gold ochre and cobalt blue, leaving white highlights. Vary the colours with Venetian red and dark washes from your palette; use the dark grey mix from step 7 for the cast shadows.

**10** ▲ **Add details** Paint dark tones on the aubergine in a mix of indigo and alizarin crimson. Use a dilute cobalt blue/alizarin crimson mix for the cast shadows on the table. Add a patch of gold ochre near the oil bottle. Now work over the painting, using existing mixes to develop tones and pull the image into focus.

**11** ▲ **Continue adding details** Paint a darker shadow on the aubergine, using a stronger version of the alizarin/indigo mix. Add deeper tones to the foreground onion, using washes based on gold ochre, Venetian red and raw umber. Define the segments of the garlic bulb with an alizarin/cobalt blue mix.

# A FEW STEPS FURTHER

*The painting is now fully resolved. Only a few tweaks are needed – darkening some of the shadows, adding highlights on the chillies and knocking back the rather stark white backdrop.*

**12** ▼ **Emphasize the shadows** Mix indigo with a touch of alizarin crimson and use it to darken some of the cast shadows. This helps the objects to 'sit' properly.

## *Express yourself*
### A hot background

A striking aspect of this pastel painting is the bright red paper it is worked on. Thickly applied pastel covers the red where necessary, but the hot colour is left showing through the glass bottle neck to suggest its transparency.

## 13▸ Add highlights with oil pastel

Use a white oil pastel to add extra highlights on the glossy surfaces of the dried chillies. The pastel gives you very precise marks and allows you to work light over dark. (Don't use the wax candle resist technique used in step 4 to add highlights to intricate subjects such as chillies. You can do it more accurately with a pastel or with white gouache.)

## 14▴ Tone the background
Mix Winsor blue and alizarin crimson to give a very pale blue-grey. Using a No. 14 round brush, wash this colour loosely over the background.

## THE FINISHED PICTURE

### A  Happy accidents
Backruns, or blooms, which often occur when working with watercolour wet-on-wet, help suggest the loose folds and texture of the red fabric backdrop.

### B  Candle lights
Highlights made with a wax candle resist have a beautiful mottled texture. Specks of paint adhere as the wax does not completely cover the paper.

### C  Reflections
The sheen of the pot was suggested by showing adjacent surfaces reflected in it, such as the golden olive oil and the dark brown and red chillies.

# Coffee and croissants

*All the necessities for a continental breakfast are arrayed in this still life. You might find a similar scene in any French café if you want to paint on location.*

▼ A spontaneous, economical style gives this watercolour painting a pleasing freshness.

Think of the painting opportunities that France has to offer and beautiful landscapes, picturesque villages and golden beaches might come to mind. But there are also paintings waiting to be made in the corner of every café. With just a few cups of coffee, a newspaper and a croissant or two, you have all the makings of an attractive and evocative still life at your disposal. Of course, you do not have to go abroad to create the ambience of the French café – you can easily do it in your own kitchen.

## Arranging the composition

Take some time over the arrangement of the objects. In the painting shown here, a newspaper, a knife and a cigarette packet are positioned at an angle in the foreground to help lead the eye into the composition. The cafetière at the centre of the table provides a focal point, and the red chair helps to give depth, as well as a bold contrast to the blue of the tablecloth.

## A simple approach

This type of subject matter lends itself to a simple, spontaneous approach – a rough pencil sketch, then a bold application of watercolour. In fact, the painting shouldn't take that much longer than the breakfast itself. Do not over-labour the colours by laying wash upon wash. And remember to be selective about where you apply the paint. To register the brightest highlights in the scene, simply leave the paper exposed.

As far as the watercolour paint is concerned, it is best to use the solid blocks that come in pans, rather than the semi-liquid variety in tubes. A selection of pans in a box is easier to transport if you are working on location. Watercolour paints in this form also allow you to work quickly, as each colour is on hand, ready to be mixed.

Sheet of 300gsm (140lb) watercolour paper

4B pencil

Brushes: Nos. 6 and 3 rounds

Mixing palette or dish

Jar of water

Paper napkin or kitchen paper

9 pan watercolours: cobalt blue; Payne's grey; burnt umber; yellow ochre; alizarin scarlet; alizarin crimson; ultramarine; cadmium yellow; viridian

## FIRST STROKES

**1 ▲ Begin the pencil sketch** With a 4B pencil, softly outline the shape of the table and chair. Then concentrate on establishing the breakfast objects. Pay particular attention to the series of ellipses formed by the cups, bowl and cafetière, and their relationship to the ellipse of the table.

**2 ◄ Re-emphasize the outlines** Give further definition to your pencil sketch. Pay attention to the perspective, especially to that of the lettering on the newspaper. Draw two converging lines, then add the letters between them. Put a minimum of detail on the sugar cubes, as this area will be left largely as exposed paper.

**3 ► Establish the tablecloth** While you do not need to draw all the squares, it is necessary to have enough lines to help with the perspective. The lines going away from you should converge slightly towards an imaginary vanishing point, while the horizontal lines should be parallel.

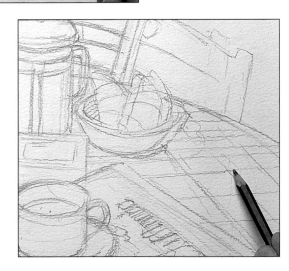

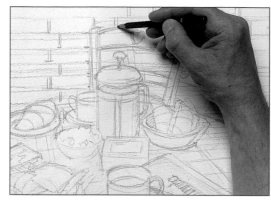

**4 ▲ Start on the background of bricks** The bricks will eventually be given only a pale wash of watercolour, so you need to put in quite a lot of detail with pencil to convey their texture. Then sit back and re-evaluate your drawing.

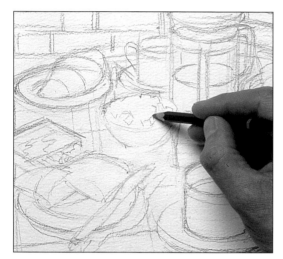

**5 ▲ Put the finishing touches on your drawing** Look over your picture and add the final details, including some definition on the edges of the sugar cubes. Remember, don't commit yourself to irreversible watercolour washes before you're totally happy with your drawing.

## RESCUING DRIED PAINT

Solid blocks of watercolour dry out very easily, especially when working on a hot summer's day. To make the colours workable again, simply hold them under running water.

**TROUBLE SHOOTER**

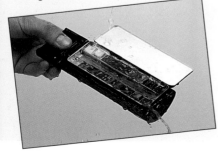

## DEVELOPING THE PICTURE

Start the painting by putting initial washes of watercolour on the main objects on the table. Then move on to the table-cloth. (If the tablecloth has small checks or an intricate pattern, be prepared to spend quite a lot of time on it – or simplify it.) Finally, go back to the objects, enhancing their colour and modelling with further washes.

**6 ▲ Begin with the dark tones** Use a weak mix of cobalt blue and Payne's grey with a No. 6 brush to render the shadows cast on the cloth. Use the same wash for the lid of the cafetière and, while it is still wet, use a strong Payne's grey to show the shadow on the right of the lid and to define the handle.

**7** ▲ **Turn to the warmer colours** Add water and burnt umber to your Payne's grey mix to render the coffee in the cafetière and cups. Add more burnt umber for the coffee on the left side of the cafetière and more Payne's grey on the shadowed side on the right. Then use a mix of burnt umber, yellow ochre and alizarin scarlet for the croissants and basket.

**8** ▲ **Paint the chair** Clean your brush thoroughly and mix together some alizarin scarlet and alizarin crimson. Use this bright-red colour to paint the chair.

**9** ▲ **Fill in the tablecloth pattern** Switch to a No. 3 brush and use a dark mix of Payne's grey and cobalt blue for the lettering on the newspaper and for the darker cast shadows. Dilute the mix for the mid tones on the cups. Clean the brush and, with a dilute mix of ultramarine, start defining the checks on the tablecloth. Use bold, long brush strokes. You need a steady hand and a degree of patience here.

**10** ▲ **Continue with the tablecloth** To get the perspective right on the vertical lines of the checked pattern, follow the guidelines you established in pencil. Use a paper napkin or a piece of kitchen paper under your hand to avoid smudging any of the lines already painted.

**11 ▲ Darken the areas in shadow** Strengthen your ultramarine mix and, using the grey washes you put in earlier as a guideline, rework the areas of the tablecloth in shadow.

**12 ▲ Overlay washes** Add a lot of water and some Payne's grey to your ultramarine mix to put in the watery colours captured in the glass ashtray. Then start building up the darker tones. Use a deep burnt umber to render the areas of coffee in shadow in the cups and cafetière. Mix up alizarin scarlet, yellow ochre and cadmium yellow for the dark glaze on the croissants. Darken the tone on the cafetière lid with Payne's grey.

## *Express yourself*
### Erasing the pencil lines

Simply by erasing the pencil marks on the painting, you will give the whole picture a fresher, more vibrant look. Much of the tone and detail of the wall was drawn in pencil. Once this is removed, the chair and table appear to leap forward towards the viewer. The bright colours seem to float and play against each other with a greater vigour. The viewer's eye is drawn across the blue tablecloth towards the areas of warmer colour.

**13 ▲ Work on the light tones** Paint in the swirling pattern on the cigarette packet using the strengthened ultramarine mix from step 11. Then add a touch of burnt umber to a mix of alizarin scarlet and alizarin crimson to put in the shaded sides of the chair. Clean your brush and use a weak mix of Payne's grey and ultramarine to paint the whitewashed wall and some of the shadows among the sugar cubes. Then add a little viridian to this mix to render the printed areas of the newspaper. Darken the mix with more Payne's grey and paint the cast shadow of the chair.

## A FEW STEPS FURTHER

*Squint at the set-up through half-closed eyes to check that you've got the tonal range right. Then give the picture greater punch by adding the darkest tones. Remember, as there is no going back with watercolour, don't add these tones until the end. Try not to spend too long tightening up the picture or you'll lose the freshness and spontaneity which are part of its appeal.*

**14** ▶ **Add some detail** Use a strong mix of Payne's grey for the dark tone on the knife; deepen it further for the detail on the cigarette packet. Mix burnt umber and alizarin crimson to show the red chair through the cafetière.

**15** ▲ **Put in the final washes** Now mix up burnt umber with a touch of yellow ochre to darken the end of the left-hand croissant in the basket (where it is caught in shadow behind the cafetière). Use the same mix for the shaded side of the basket.

## THE FINISHED PICTURE

**A Less is more**
A few dabs of grey for some shadowed sides of the sugar cubes was all that was needed to suggest their shape. The same technique was used for the cigarettes.

**B Cast shadows**
The artist used a considerably darker blue in the shadow areas of the tablecloth to prevent the objects from appearing to float above the table.

**C Delicate touches**
Changes of tone and colour were subtly applied to the ashtray to capture the reflections of the tablecloth and the cafetière in the glass.

# Brilliant anemones

*Use alizarin crimson and brilliant violet gouache paints to bring out the vivid colours of these anemones.*

▶ **The unusual textural effects in this floral still life are achieved with a wax-resist technique and by overdrawing with water-soluble painting crayons.**

As she painted, the artist decided to alter the composition she had initially set up (left). The red flowers were still painted at the centre of the display – with the bold colour pulling the eye into the composition – but the other flowers were more widely spaced, so they create a roughly elliptical shape around the red ones. This encourages the eye to travel around the whole of the display. Note also how the glass vase with its sharp verticals pleasingly offsets the natural shapes of the flowers.

A nemones, with their beautiful and vivid colours, look wonderful arranged casually in a vase and simply cry out to be painted. This still life, with its mixed-media approach, is a particularly unusual interpretation of these well-loved flowers.

### Unusual approach

The artist began this gouache study in the conventional way, laying down colours from lights to darks. However, she didn't stop there – instead, she chose to give the picture more character with different methods and materials.

The mottled texture seen on the vase and background was created by rubbing a household candle over these areas to act as a resist. The picture was given a lift by adding bold lines of water-soluble crayon in white and pale blue. The result is a dense, richly textured work.

### YOU WILL NEED

Piece of rough 300gsm (140lb) watercolour paper 46 x 38cm (18 x 15in)

Green water-soluble coloured pencil

9 gouache paints: lemon yellow; cerulean blue; ultramarine; cadmium red; cadmium red pale hue; brilliant violet; alizarin crimson; indigo; Winsor green

Brushes: No. 16 wash brush; No. 8 round; No. 2 rigger

Mixing palette or dish

White household candle

2 water-soluble painting crayons: white; pale blue

## FIRST STEPS

**1** ▼ **Rough in the flowers** Water-soluble pencils are good drawing tools as they wash out as soon as you paint over them. Use a green one to plot the position of the vase, the flowers and the tablecloth.

**2** ▼ **Wash in the background** Load a No. 16 wash brush with clean water and 'paint' over the lightest areas of the composition – around the vase and the tops of the flowers. Then go over these wetted areas with lemon yellow gouache. Painting in this way, rather than simply diluting the yellow in the palette, creates a lovely pale hue.

**3** ▼ **Pick out some leaves** With the same brush, put in some green accents with mixes of lemon yellow and cerulean blue to start suggesting particular stems and leaves. Let the leaves bleed into the yellow for a softer, more naturalistic effect.

**4** ▶ **Outline the flower-heads** Select a No. 8 round brush for the more delicate details and, as before, work first with just water, then paint over the moistened areas with your colour. Use cerulean blue to outline the vase and form the shapes of the flowers, including their dark centres.

**5** ▲ **Switch to a cooler blue** Change back to the No. 16 wash brush to put in some of the shadows with ultramarine. Apply directional brush strokes, painting a shadow to the left of the vase and adding a few darker touches to the tablecloth.

**6** ▲ **Start with the reds** Using the No. 8 round brush, paint the red flowers with cadmium red and cadmium red pale hue. Vary the colour strengths to give the petals form.

## DEVELOPING THE PICTURE

Continue adding vivid mixes of gouache to the anemones to bring out the intense colours of their petals. Define their outlines and add details such as the flower centres with a No. 2 rigger brush.

**8 ◄ Mix mauve tones** The blue flowers have touches of mauve in them. To create these tones, mix brilliant violet with ultramarine, and apply in varying strengths to the petals with the No. 8 round. Paint the flower to the right of the arrangement first.

**7 ▲ Paint a pinkish-purple flower** Use brilliant violet and the wash brush for the dark tones on the central flower, working inwards from a dark outline. Wash in a little alizarin crimson for the pinker touches on the top petals.

## EXPERT ADVICE
## Soften the colours

Create softer tones on the anemones by first painting the petals in your chosen colour, then brushing over them with water. Quickly blot the loosened pigment with paper tissue or kitchen paper to lift some of the colour away.

**9 ▼ Define the edges of the petals** Paint the blue flower to the right of the pinkish-purple one, using the mix from step 8. Now, with the tip of the No. 2 rigger brush, paint tiny dots of indigo paint around the centre of the blue flower. With the same brush and indigo, define the edges of the pinkish-purple flower petals.

**10** ▼ **Continue painting the flowers** Move from one flower head to the next, painting and defining the petals as before. To strengthen the white flowers, add touches of the mauve mix from step 8 (applying water first). Outline the petals of the lower white flower in cerulean blue.

**11** ▶ **Work on the vase** There is a suggestion of water in the vase, but it needs to be strengthened. With the No. 16 wash brush, paint a slash of cerulean blue inside the right-hand corner to suggest a shadow. Add a few lines of Winsor green for the stems, then accentuate the base of the vase with a strong line of cerulean blue.

**12** ▼ **Create a sense of space** Add a shadow at the base of the vase with a broad slash of cerulean. Darken the fabric folds with a cerulean/ ultramarine mix. Strengthen the background with vertical strokes of Winsor green and ultramarine.

# Express yourself

## A square format

Experiment with different formats and viewpoints. Here the flowers take centre stage, radiating upwards and outwards. The view is more stylized than realistic – the anemones are framed by a square within a square, rather than sitting firmly and palpably on a table. The smaller square could be read as a window or simply as an artistic device.

**13** ▼ **Strengthen the background** To add warmth and energy to the painting, strengthen the background with a wash of lemon yellow. Work carefully around the flower-heads.

**14** ▾ **Paint over wax** Rub a white household candle over the vase and lower right-hand corner to form a resist. Mix indigo with a touch of ultramarine and apply this thickly over the waxed surface. Notice the grainy effect that results from the wax repelling the paint.

## WAX-RESIST EFFECTS

You can achieve richly textured effects by painting gouache over a resist of candle wax. Experiment with washes of different strengths.

▲ An indigo/ultramarine mix applied over white candle wax (see step 14).

▲ Candle wax over a dried yellow wash, overlaid with an indigo/ultramarine wash (see step 15).

**15** ▾ **Apply a second layer of wax** Continue applying wax to sections of the still life. Work your way all around the arrangement from the top left-hand corner to the right of the vase and below it. Now paint a dark indigo/ultramarine glaze over the wax.

**16** ◂ **Strengthen the background** The dark tones provide depth and solidity. Continue building up shadows on the right and around the edges with a stronger indigo/ultramarine wash.

## A FEW STEPS FURTHER

*Having built up the area to the right of the flowers, it now appears somewhat dark and lacking in texture. The surface of the table could be improved, too, by putting in some creases and points of visual interest.*

**17** ◂ **Draw a white line** Using a white water-soluble painting crayon, draw a strong vertical line behind the top right-hand flowers to highlight the background.

**18** ◄ **Add more highlights** Still using the white painting crayon, add a few short strokes along the edge of the vase. Then rub the crayon over the table top to the left of the vase and wash over it with clean water to make the area appear lighter.

**19** ▲ **Use a blue crayon** Add more dramatic lines in white, both on and around the vase, then switch to a pale blue painting crayon. Put a strong blue accent on the edge of the vase, and softer ones in the shadows.

# THE FINISHED PICTURE

**A Focal point**
The tall white anemone, reaching up above the others and silhouetted by the dark background, forms a focal point in the composition.

**B Light and dark**
Exaggerating the dark shadows on the right gives the picture punch and helps to make the petals stand forward.

**C Illusion of water**
Two lines of crayon – one blue, one white – suggest the surface of the water seen through glass.

# Birman temple cat

*Photographs are an invaluable reference source for painting an animal. Choose the best background and pose, then combine them for a great composition.*

▼ **The strong colours and shapes in the background set off the fluffy texture and pale tones of the cat's fur.**

Family pets are challenging but very rewarding subjects to paint. They do, however, have a habit of getting up and strolling away just as you're about to start painting. So, unless you have an unusually obliging specimen, your best option is to use photos to help you.

A danger with painting from photos is that you can end up with a picture that looks rather flat and two-dimensional. Purists often reject the practice and claim that they can tell when something has been painted from a photo because it lacks vitality. The secret is not to base your picture entirely on your photographs, but to use them more as a springboard for your work while also referring to your actual pet.

## The Birman legend

An unusual breed of cat – the Birman temple cat – was chosen for this project.

### YOU WILL NEED

| | |
|---|---|
| Piece of 300gsm (140lb) NOT watercolour paper 34 x 38cm (13½ x 15in) | Dyke brown; zinc white; raw umber; cobalt blue; scarlet lake; yellow ochre |
| 2B pencil | Brushes: Nos. 4, 10 and 1 rounds |
| 7 gouache paints: ivory black; Van | Mixing palette or dish |

The story goes that this breed originally had yellow eyes and white fur, and guarded the Temple of Lao-Tsun in Myanmar (formerly Burma). One day, the temple was attacked and the head priest killed. At the moment of the priest's death, his favourite cat placed its feet on him and its markings changed for ever. Its fur took on a golden cast, its eyes turned blue and its face, legs and tail became the colour of the earth. However, the cat's paws, having touched the priest, remained white as a symbol of purity.

The Birman temple cat used as a model here is true to this distinctive colouring. It has been painted from two different photos as well as from life. The photo of the cat sitting on the wooden floor shows the better pose, but the more interesting background in terms of colour is the one with the cat on the sofa, so the artist combined the two in her painting.

## Blending with gouache

A small palette of gouache colours is used for this exciting project. Gouache works equally well for delicate areas such as the cat's fur and for the strong, bold background. Used wet-on-wet, the paint creates areas of colour that blend softly together.

## FIRST STEPS

**1 ▼ Make a pencil sketch** Using the photograph showing the cat in a sitting pose as a guide, make a sketch with a 2B pencil. This species is characteristically fluffy, so the front body, back body and head form roughly circular shapes.

### EXPERT ADVICE
### Get the proportions right

Use your pencil to gauge the proportions of the cat. Align the tip with the top of the head and note where the bottom of the paws fall on the pencil. Use this measurement to check the breadth of the body. You'll find that, ignoring the tail, the two are roughly the same, so make sure your drawn cat is about as tall as it is broad.

**2 ▲ Establish the darkest areas** Make a mix of ivory black with just a touch of Van Dyke brown. Using a No. 4 round brush, start painting the darkest tones – the face (apart from the cheeks) and the bottom of the legs and tail.

**3 ▲ Vary the tones** Add a little zinc white to your brown mix and finish off the tail and front legs. Use this lighter tone for the cheeks, too, taking special care around the eyes.

**4** ▼ **Work on the light tones** Change to a No. 10 round brush and make a thin, pale mix of zinc white with a hint of raw umber. Use this to paint the cat's body. For the darker tones, add a little more of the raw umber to the mix.

**5** ▼ **Paint wet-on-wet** Referring to the photograph, build up tonal variations within the fur. Work wet-on-wet with various dilute mixes of white and raw umber, adding darker browns over lighter ones. The colours will bleed into each other, giving the fur a sense of softness so that the cat looks suitably fluffy.

**6** ▼ **Change the background** Allow about 15 minutes for the cat to dry. Now put your photo aside and look at the other one, where the cat is surrounded by colourful cushions. Use this as reference for the background. Still using the No. 10 brush, add slashes of strong cobalt blue both above and below the cat.

**7** ▶ **Add some red** The blue changes the composition entirely, framing your subject and throwing it into relief. Add an equally strong red to the right of the blue, using scarlet lake with a touch of Van Dyke brown. Paint carefully around the fur so as to not disturb any of the creamy body colour.

**8** ◀ **Paint the final cushion** On the left is a cushion patterned with browns, gold and blue. Use yellow ochre mixed with a little white for the gold areas and, while this is still wet, add a thick band of cobalt blue. Paint the darker areas wet-on-wet with various mixes of raw umber, white and black.

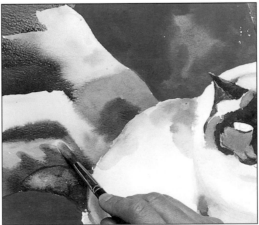

## DEVELOPING THE PICTURE

The completed background forms a striking contrast to the shape and colouring of the cat. Now turn your attention back to the cat itself and start to develop its features and the texture of its fluffy, silky fur.

**9 ◄ Paint the eyes** Use the No. 4 brush for finer details such as the eyes. Birman cats have pale blue eyes, so mix up a dilute cobalt blue for these. Use pure black for the pupils to make them really stand out.

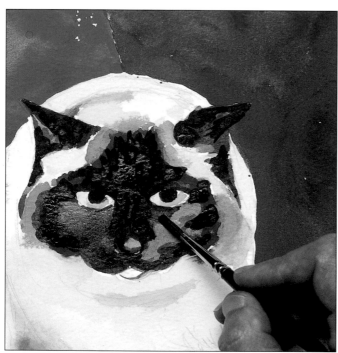

**10 ▲ Strengthen the face** Make a very dark mix of black and Van Dyke brown. Using the No. 4 brush, accentuate the darkness of the face, particularly around the eyes.

**11 ▲ Define the fur** With the No. 4 brush, paint a pale gold ruff around the cat's face with a mix of yellow ochre and white. To give the fur a more downy appearance, apply the pale mix from step 4 with the very tip of the brush to paint individual hairs along the right-hand side of the body.

**12** ▶ **Add tonal variation to the blue** Continue defining individual hairs above the cat's head and along the contour of its back, varying the tones by using some of the mixes from step 5. Finally, add shadows to the blue cushion with a mix of cobalt blue and black to make it appear softer and more luxurious.

## *Express yourself*
### Change of scenery

The original background of wooden floorboards was used for this interpretation of the Birman temple cat. The brown tones harmonize well with the neutral colours of the cat's fur, but the more colourful background of the step-by-step project complements the character of the cat.

## A FEW STEPS FURTHER

*The picture is almost complete. As a finishing touch, add a few highlights to the cat's facial features to help liven it up and make it stand out more against the richly coloured background.*

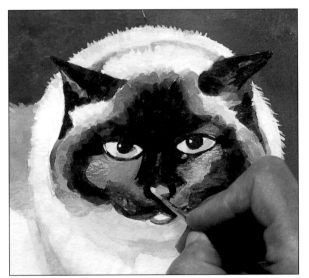

**13** ▲ **Add highlights** Add a spot of white to each pupil to show reflected light. Make a pale grey mix from white plus touches of black and cobalt blue, and paint the highlights on the fur under the eyes. For the tip of the nose, add more white to the mix.

**14** ▼ **Create shadows** As the composition is built up from a combination of two photos, you'll need to use your imagination to create cast shadows on the cushions. Paint some dark shadows around the cat's paws and lower body, using a mix of cobalt blue and black.

**15** ▲ **Draw the whiskers** Finally, use a No. 1 round brush and the pale grey mix from step 13 to draw in the delicate, sensitive hairs of the whiskers.

# THE FINISHED PICTURE

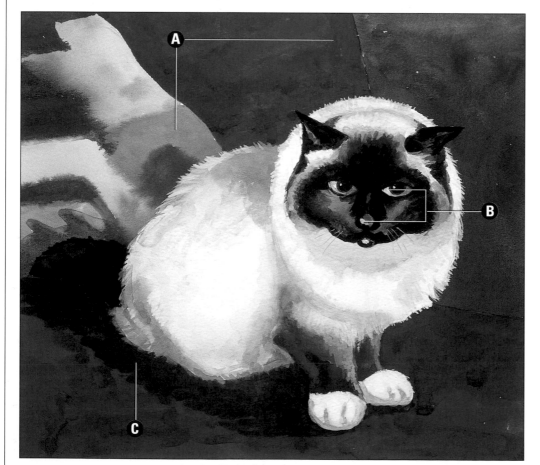

**A Bold background**
The bold swathes of colour in the background are left largely undefined, so as not to distract from the cat – the focus of the picture.

**B White highlights**
Dots of pure white on the eyes and pale grey on the tip of the nose suggest moistness and add an important touch of realism.

**C Areas of shadow**
The dark shadows around the cat's hindquarters prevent it from appearing to float above the surface of the cushion.

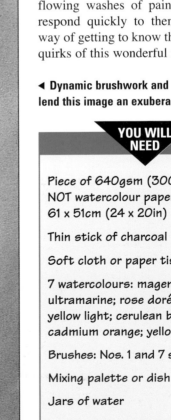

# Potted Hyacinths

*Exploit the fluidity and expressiveness of watercolour to the full in this painting of potted hyacinths.*

Perhaps you are worried that your watercolour paintings look too 'timid'. It's worth trying some bold experiments now and again to inject excitement into your work and increase your confidence with the medium. Learn to explore and exploit the fluidity of watercolour for all it is worth; you have to work with the nature of the medium and not against it.

This painting shows an obvious delight in the aqueous quality of pure watercolour. The artist applies the paint in great sweeps of saturated colour, taking advantage of the marks and textures that form as the paint flows, settles and dries, and allowing the paint to do much of the work.

## Free movement

Use a large sheet of heavyweight paper, and paint standing up. This allows you to put more energy into your picture. Hold the brush near the end of the handle for freedom of movement. Use vivid colours and leave some areas of white paper to set them off to maximum advantage. Be ready for accidents when controlling flowing washes of paint and learn to respond quickly to them. It's a great way of getting to know the qualities and quirks of this wonderful medium.

◄ **Dynamic brushwork and bold colours lend this image an exuberant quality.**

▼ **YOU WILL NEED**

Piece of 640gsm (300lb) NOT watercolour paper 61 x 51cm (24 x 20in)

Thin stick of charcoal

Soft cloth or paper tissue

7 watercolours: magenta; ultramarine; rose doré; cadmium yellow light; cerulean blue; cadmium orange; yellow-green

Brushes: Nos. 1 and 7 squirrel mops

Mixing palette or dish

Jars of water

## FIRST STEPS

**1** ▶ **Make a drawing** Use a thin stick of charcoal to make a light outline drawing of the hyacinths and pots. Suggest some of the individual blooms, but avoid putting in too much detail. Any loose charcoal dust on the surface of the drawing will dull your subsequent watercolour washes, so knock it back by lightly flicking (not rubbing) it with a soft cloth or a paper tissue.

**2** ◀ **Start painting the hyacinths** Prepare a fluid wash of bluish purple mixed from magenta, ultramarine and a little rose doré. Touch in some of the individual hyacinth petals, using the tip of a No. 1 mop brush and letting the strokes bleed into each other. Vary the hues by adding more blue or red to the mix.

# *Express yourself*
## White flowers

An interesting feature of this watercolour is the hazy, black outline defining the plant and pot. This was achieved by drawing with a dip pen and Indian ink on watercolour paper, then taking off most of the ink with a wet sponge. Before the paper dried out, washes of colour were applied wet-on-wet.

## EXPERT ADVICE
## Versatile mop brushes

Squirrel mops come in a range of different sizes and combine an incredible paint-holding capacity with a very soft hair that has the ability to be moulded. Use the belly and heel of the brush for broad washes and wet-on-wet passages (right). The tip comes to a very fine point for rendering details and hard edges (left).

## DEVELOPING THE PICTURE

As you continue with the step-by-step, you will be using large amounts of fluid paint. Leave plenty of mixing room in the middle of the palette and don't forget to change your water frequently to keep your colours fresh.

**3** ▶ **Paint the leaves and pots** Mix a fluid wash of cadmium yellow light with a little cerulean blue. Fill in the hyacinth leaves with lots of juicy colour. Use pure cadmium orange to paint the terra-cotta pots. While this is still wet, brush in the shadows on the pots with vertical strokes of ultramarine. Leave the painting to dry.

**4 ▼ Start on the background** Prepare a big wash of cadmium yellow light with a tiny amount of cerulean blue. Change to a No. 7 mop brush and, working quickly, make broad, sweeping strokes that surround the hyacinths. Use plenty of wash and work with the belly and heel of the brush, holding it near the end of the handle for maximum freedom of movement.

**5 ▲ Add more washes to the background** Work some of the same wash down into the spaces between the three hyacinths, leaving a rough border of untouched white paper around the group as a whole. Add yellow-green to the wash to make a zingy, acid green. Fill in the outer edges of the paper with broad sweeps of the brush.

**6 ◄ Develop the leaves** Fill more white space between the hyacinths with the acid-green colour, leaving a ragged 'halo' of white around each one. Now change to the No. 1 mop brush and develop the forms of the leaves with transparent shadows mixed from varied tones of yellow-green and ultramarine. Add a touch of magenta to the mix for the warm shadows inside the leaves.

**7** ▼ **Add background texture** Using mixes of magenta, ultramarine and rose doré, develop the hyacinth blooms with touches of deeper tone applied with the brush tip. Make up a medium-toned, fluid wash of cerulean blue and go over the outer part of the background with circular sweeps of the No. 7 mop brush. Leave to dry.

# A FEW STEPS FURTHER

*By working boldly with the luminous, fluid watercolour, you have created a simple yet stunning image. A few final refinements will complete the picture.*

**8** ▼ **Brighten the pots** Now that the background is filled in, the pots look a little pale. Add a further wash of cadmium orange to intensify their colour. The paint will spread and form hard edges as it dries.

**9** ▲ **Final flourish** Sweep an intense wash of yellow-green and cerulean blue around the outer edges. This slightly darker tone helps to 'frame' the image.

# THE FINISHED PICTURE

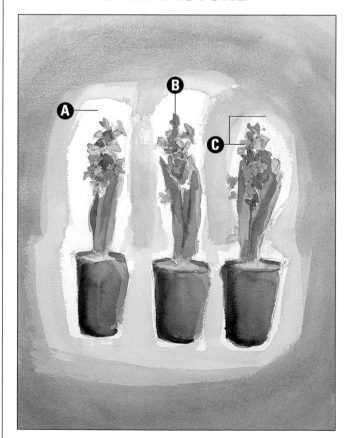

**A Halo of white**
The white space around the flowers has an important positive presence, drawing our eye to each plant.

**B Intense colour**
Vivid yet transparent pigments create the intense colour of the flowers, while at the same time capturing their physical delicacy.

**C Hard and soft**
Hard edges contrast with soft, fluid washes, creating textural interest and enlivening the surface of the picture.

# Still life with melon

*Try a direct, 'no-drawing' approach to watercolour painting to achieve a bold, spontaneous effect.*

For centuries, artists have used fruit and vegetables as an inspiration for still-life paintings. Works range from the lavish to the humble, from exotic fruit tumbling off silver salvers to partially peeled potatoes on scrubbed wooden tables.

Whatever your taste, you will find that fruit and vegetables make extremely versatile subjects. Fortunately, they are also easy to get hold of and a quick trip to the local market can set you up with an extraordinary range of shapes, colours and textures with which to compose your picture.

Here, the artist chose a melon for the textural detail of its seeds, a vine of cherry tomatoes to create interesting negative shapes and a lemon and an aubergine for their strong colours and harmonious, curvaceous forms.

## Fresh approach

To paint this colourful arrangement, try taking a fresh approach to a classical subject. Apply the watercolour without a preliminary pencil drawing – a bold method that produces equally bold results. Use big brushes to keep your work immediate and lively, and avoid over-working the colours. Although a small brush was used to define the melon seeds, fine lines and details can generally be painted quickly and easily using the tip of a Chinese brush.

▼ **Bold application of watercolour brings out the strong, clear colours of the fruit and makes them stand out from the background.**

## FIRST STEPS

**1 ▲ Position the melon** Using a Chinese brush, start by boldly blocking in the shapes of the melon flesh in dilute gamboge yellow. Make sure the proportions and positions are correct.

**2 ▶ Paint the tomato stalks** With the tip of the Chinese brush, paint the main tomato stalk with a mixture of gamboge yellow and Winsor green. Judge the correct position of the stalk by relating it to the painted melon, taking care to leave unpainted spaces for the tomatoes.

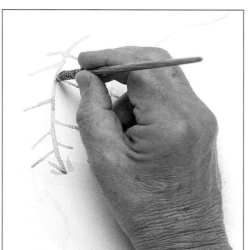

## YOU WILL NEED

Piece of 300 gsm (140lb) NOT watercolour paper 56 x 76cm (22 x 30in)

Brushes: Chinese brush; No. 3 soft round; 25mm (1in) soft flat

19 watercolours: gamboge yellow; Winsor green; lemon yellow; ivory black; cadmium orange; raw sienna; emerald green;

scarlet lake; viridian; burnt sienna; raw umber; cadmium red; Winsor violet; permanent rose; burnt umber; cobalt blue; alizarin crimson; ultramarine; sap green

Mixing dish

Rags and newspaper

Masking tape

Old toothbrush

**3 ▲ Add the lemon** Paint the lemon in pure lemon yellow, leaving a patch of white to represent the highlight. Using the tip of the brush, dot in the dappled peel texture on the highlight. Outline the right-hand edge with a stronger lemon yellow mix.

## RESCUING HIGHLIGHTS

**TROUBLE SHOOTER**

Leave unpainted paper for the white highlights on shiny fruit and vegetables. If you forget to do this, move quickly before the paint dries and create a highlight by soaking up the colour with a dry cotton bud.

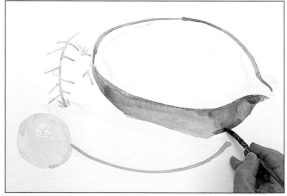

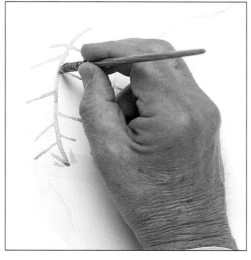

**4 ▲ Develop the melon** Allow the colours to dry, then outline the melon shapes with a strong mix of Winsor green with a little added ivory black and cadmium orange. Add more water and a little more orange to the mixture, and flood this into the centre of the melon half, allowing the colour to bleed into the darker tone.

**5 ▼ Add the melon seeds** Paint the shaded edge of the melon flesh in a mixture of Winsor green and lemon yellow. Add the seeds to the segment of melon in the foreground in gamboge yellow and raw sienna, leaving the pith as an unpainted white shape.

**6 ▼ Paint the tomatoes** Paint a mixture of emerald green and lemon yellow around the edge of the melon. Add three tomatoes in washes of cadmium orange and scarlet lake, leaving highlights unpainted. Paint the half-melon's seeds in mixes of raw sienna, cadmium orange and gamboge yellow.

## DEVELOP THE PICTURE

You will need to change to a smaller brush to put in some of the detail. It is important, however, to keep the painting generally bold and broad.

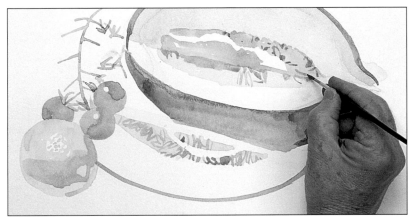

**7 ▲ Add details** Complete the tomato stalks in gamboge yellow and Winsor green. Paint the shadow on the lemon in gamboge yellow with small amounts of viridian and raw sienna. Change to a No. 3 soft round brush and define the seeds in mixtures of raw sienna, burnt sienna and raw umber.

**8 ▲ Develop the colours** With the Chinese brush, block in the remaining tomatoes in cadmium orange and cadmium red, painting around the green stalks. Add the dark stripes to the outside of the melon, painting these as broken lines of Winsor green and raw sienna.

## *Express yourself*
## Fruit substitute

You can change the emphasis of the still life by substituting one fruit or vegetable for another. In this painting of a similar subject, a watermelon dominates the colour scheme. Its bright pink centre draws the eye more than the pale green flesh of the melon used in the project. The grapes play the same role as the tomatoes in the step-by-step, creating intricate detail and interesting negative shapes. Try, too, altering the background slightly, putting in additional colours and textures.

**9** ◄ **Paint the aubergine** Block in the aubergine in Winsor violet with a touch of ivory black and permanent rose, painting carefully around the tomatoes and stems. Leave the jagged highlights unpainted, referring closely to the subject to find their exact shapes.

**10** ► **Block in the shadows** Change to a 25mm (1in) soft flat brush and block in the shadows around the fruit and plate in a mixture of Winsor violet, burnt sienna and a little black. Paint the shadows on the white fabric in a diluted version of the same colour. Take the same diluted colour over the highlights on the aubergine.

**11 ▼ Paint the background** Loosely paint the glass bottle with a mixture of Winsor violet and burnt umber, leaving the lower half of the bottle unpainted to indicate the pale stone behind. Block in the background and stone with bold strokes, using dark and pale mixtures of raw sienna, ivory black and Winsor violet.

**EXPERT ADVICE**
**Composition check**

As you have not made an initial drawing, check your composition as you progress. Choose a support larger than you want the finished picture to be, then cut a card mount. By moving the mount around on the painting from time to time during the early stages, you can choose a suitable composition at any time as work progresses.

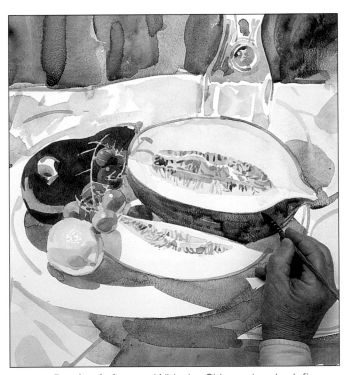

## A FEW STEPS FURTHER

*The watercolour is virtually finished, but you might wish to add one or two finishing touches before putting down your brushes. For example, the background and the stone are possibly rather too similar in tone and texture.*

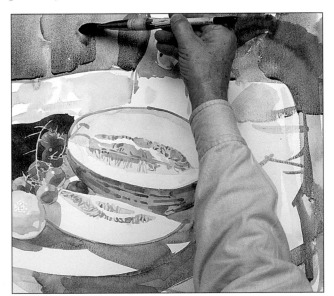

**12 ▲ Darken the background** Working in bold, broad strokes, strengthen the background with dark washes of burnt umber mixed with ivory black and a little Winsor violet. Use the same mixtures to emphasize the shadow around the right-hand side of the stone.

**13 ▲ Develop dark tones** With the Chinese brush, define the motif and reflections on the bottle in a mix of cobalt blue and ivory black. Paint alizarin crimson shadows on the tomatoes and add a cool shadow to the lemon in a mixture of gamboge yellow, black and ultramarine. Emphasize the melon seeds in mixtures of raw and burnt sienna, and darken the outside of the melon in sap green and black.

**14** ▼ **Mask the picture** Prepare to add a spattered texture to the surface of the stone by first protecting the rest of the painting with old rags and newspaper. Stick these down with masking tape, positioning the tape carefully so that it protects the edges of the plate, cloth and bottle.

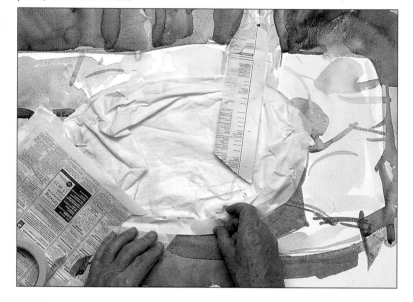

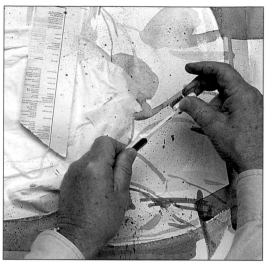

**15** ▲ **Spatter the stone** To spatter, mix a wash of sap green and burnt sienna. Dip an old toothbrush into the diluted colour and hold the loaded brush a little way above the area to be spattered. Pull the bristles back and flick the colour across the paper, repeating this until the stone is covered with a speckled texture.

# THE FINISHED PICTURE

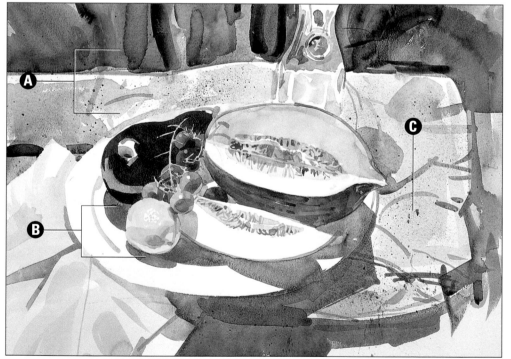

**A Muted background**
The background was painted in dark, neutral colours which do not compete with the central subjects: the brightly coloured fruit and shiny aubergine.

**B Shadow shapes**
The artist used cool violet-grey shadows on the plate to reflect curved shapes within the subject and play a positive role in the overall composition.

**C Speckled stone**
Spattered texture on the stone is light and minimal – just enough to differentiate it from the smooth cloth. It does not detract from the main elements in the composition.

# Trout in watercolour

*Use a combination of pure watercolour and water-soluble pencils to capture the shimmering colours of these rainbow trout.*

The streamlined body shapes and iridescent colours of rainbow trout make them an absorbing subject. Arrange the pair of fish on a white plate – the austere background highlights their simple shapes and delicate hues. A more dramatic background would be distracting. If necessary, tilt the plate to provide you with a high viewpoint, as this will give a strong composition. Spray the fish with water from time to time, using a plant mister, to keep them looking fresh and glossy. Organize the lighting carefully – you should be able to see the details clearly, but strong shadows will add impact.

## Combining media

This is an ideal subject for a mixed media technique. Wet-in-wet washes of watercolour are ideal for the delicate blushes of colour on the skin of the fish. Wet the paper with clean water first, then flow in very pale washes to begin with. Increase the intensity of the colour in the subsequent layers. This method of working gives you the control that you need to achieve a realistic look for the reflective bodies of the trout. When the basic forms are established, you can apply detail and texture with water-soluble pencils. In this project, the artist exploits an unusual technique to depict the characteristic speckling.

▼ **You will need a delicate touch and a subtle palette of watercolours to convey the iridescent effect on the bodies of these rainbow trout.**

**YOU WILL NEED**

Piece of 555gsm (260lb) NOT watercolour paper

HB pencil

Masking fluid plus old brush and soap

Brushes: Nos. 10 and 7 rounds

8 watercolours: Winsor blue (if unavailable, use phthalo blue); permanent rose; viridian; ultramarine blue; burnt umber; cadmium yellow; cadmium red; permanent violet

Tissue paper

Craft knife

7 water-soluble coloured pencils: dark blue; soft green; grey; light blue; bright blue; dark brown; red

## FIRST STROKES

**1 ▶ Draw the subject**
Start by making a careful drawing of the fish and the plate, using an HB pencil. Notice how the artist has arranged the fish on a slight diagonal to produce a dynamic composition. If they had been horizontal, the image would have been quite static.

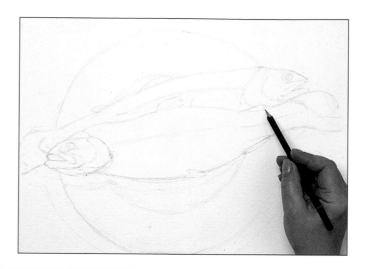

**2 ▶ Mask the highlights** The silvery highlights of the fish scales are represented by the white of the paper. Protect these areas with masking fluid while you lay on washes of colour. Use an old brush and rub a bit of soap into it before you dip it into the masking fluid – it will be easier to clean later. Place masking fluid over all the brightest parts of the fish. Wash the brush. Leave the mask to dry thoroughly.

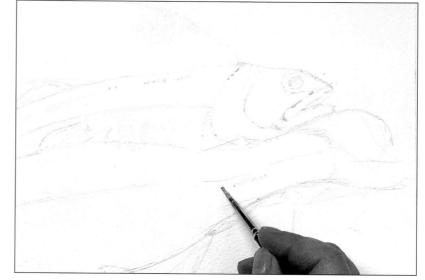

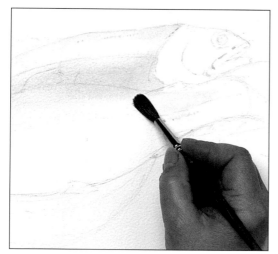

**3 ▲ Apply the first washes** Wet a No. 10 brush and dampen the two fish. Lay a very pale wash of Winsor blue along the back of the top fish. While this is still wet, lay a wash of permanent rose below it. Wash viridian along the back of the lower fish, overlapping the rose to make grey. Place a band of rose along the middle of the lower fish, then mix ultramarine blue and rose for the pale violet on its belly.

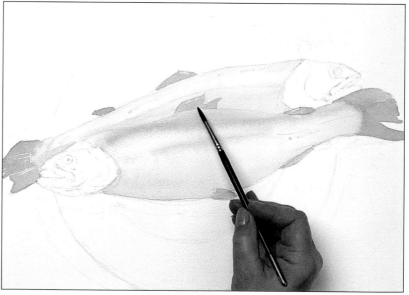

**4 ▲ Paint the tail and fins** Allow the first washes to dry completely. Mix Winsor blue and burnt umber to give an intense, warm grey for the tails and fins. Apply the colour carefully, using the tip of the No. 10 brush. Leave to dry.

**5**▼ **Paint the plate** The white, glazed surface of the plate picks up colours reflected from the adjacent surfaces, including the fish. Apply very pale washes of permanent rose, cadmium yellow and Winsor blue, allowing the washes to blend and bleed into one another to create a delicate, pearly effect. Allow these washes to dry.

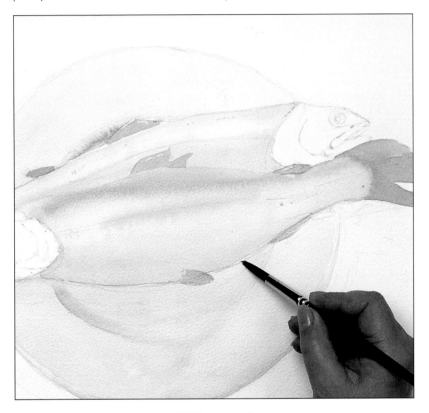

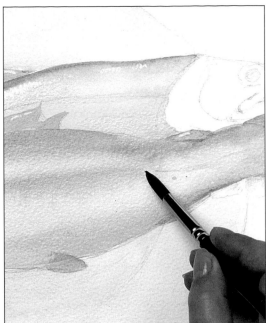

**6**▲ **Strengthen the colours** Moisten the fish with water, avoiding the overlap where you need a crisp edge. Wash a mix of Winsor blue and permanent rose along the back of the top fish, adding viridian beneath it. Flood bands of cadmium yellow on each side of the rose stripe on the lower fish. Paint a little of the pale violet mix from step 3 on the belly. Deepen the rose stripe on the side of the fish and darken its back with a mix of Winsor blue and burnt umber.

## *Express yourself*

### A new composition

Experiment with composition whenever you can. Very small adjustments can entirely change the character and impact of an image. Here, a single fish is displayed on a plain white plate. By arranging it so that it fills the picture area from corner to corner, the artist has given the image energy and has emphasized the graphic qualities of the subject.

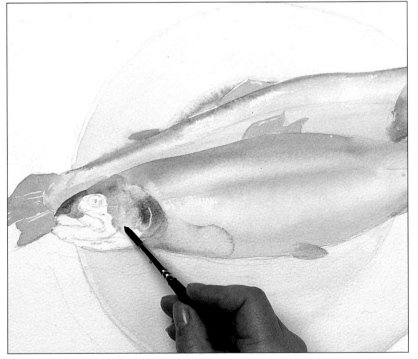

**7**▲ **Paint the heads** Add a touch of burnt umber to Winsor blue and use this for the dark areas on the right-hand fish's head. Working wet-in-wet, apply cadmium yellow and permanent rose. Develop the head on the left in the same way, using the mixed grey, permanent rose, burnt umber and a little cadmium red. Allow to dry thoroughly.

## DEVELOPING THE PICTURE

The image has been established using a series of wet-in-wet washes. Now, the water-soluble pencils will come into their own. You can use them to draw details such as the eyes, to add small areas of intense colour and to develop textures using a variety of techniques.

**8 ▲ Apply texture** Re-wet the fish, then blot the surface with a tissue so that it is just damp. Using a craft knife, scrape specks of pigment from a dark blue pencil tip over the backs of both fish, dusting them with granules of colour. Repeat with soft green and grey pencils.

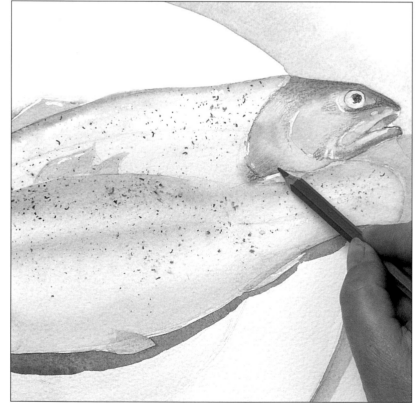

**9 ▲ Paint the shadows** Mix ultramarine and permanent rose to create a cool violet for the cast shadows. Apply this wash with the No. 10 brush, working underneath the lower fish and around the outside of the plate and crisping up the outlines at the same time. Using the same wash, add the shadows cast by the tails. Notice how the shadows give the image a three-dimensional feeling and establish the horizontal surface on which the plate is resting.

### EXPERT ADVICE
#### Customize your palette

If you want to build up intense colours using water-soluble coloured pencils, make a palette on a piece of scrap paper. Hatch patches of the shades you want to use. You can dissolve the colours with a brush dipped in water, then transfer them to the image. This method allows you to control the intensity of the wash.

**10 ▲ Add details in water-soluble coloured pencil** Lay a very pale wash of Winsor blue over the background at the top of the image. While it is still wet, introduce touches of cadmium yellow and permanent violet to create a delicately variegated wash. Use a dark blue water-soluble pencil to create the dark pupil of the eye and the shading on the head of each fish. Go over these with grey pencil. Use this pencil to draw the details of the mouth and the eye socket. Take a light blue pencil and apply hatched shading within the mouth, along the cheek and under the head.

## 11 ▶ Blend the pencil colours

Using a No. 7 brush dipped in water, start to blend the water-soluble pencil colours. Work carefully, as the pigment in some water-soluble pencils is very intense and might overwhelm the subject. If the washes you create are too saturated, blot the surface gently with a tissue.

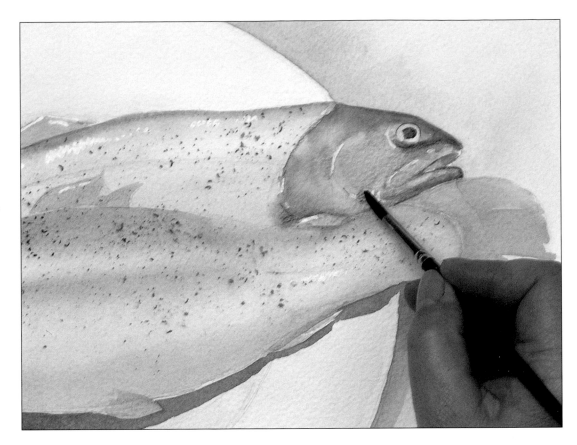

**12** ▲ **Tighten up the image** Using the paper palette method, define the back of the top fish with bright blue pigment picked up on a brush, and paint the fins with dark brown. When the painting is dry, remove the film of masking fluid.

## A FEW STEPS FURTHER

*Deciding when your painting is finished is one of the most difficult decisions you have to make. The trick is to add a touch more detail and texture without jeopardizing the spontaneity of the image.*

**13** ▲ **Refine the outlines** With the dark blue water-soluble pencil, redraw the backs of the fish and the outlines of the fins. Using the blue and grey water-soluble pencils, draw spots along the back of the fish to suggest the larger dappled marks on their backs.

**14** ▲ **Draw the scales** With a red pencil, draw a regular cross-hatched pattern along the side of the fish to suggest its scaly surface. If you create just a small area of detail, the eye will fill in the rest.

**15** ▲ **Darken the cast shadow** Hatch in more scales in shades of blue and grey. Using the No. 7 brush and ultramarine blue with a touch of permanent rose, intensify the colour of the shadow cast by the plate.

# THE FINISHED PICTURE

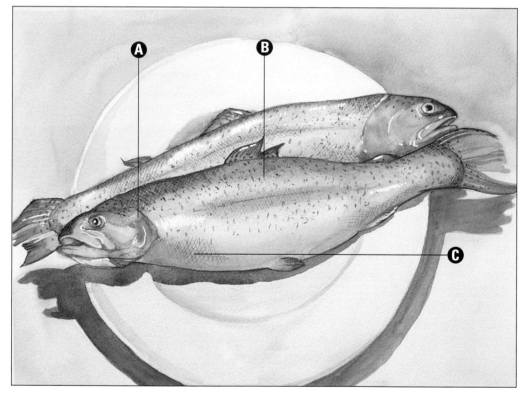

**A Delicate wet-in-wet washes**
By applying the washes to damp paper, the artist allowed the colours to flow into each other to create subtle colour blends. These perfectly captured the iridescence of the skin of the trout.

**B Speckled pattern**
The dots of colour on the fish were created by scraping water-soluble pencil on to damp paper, and by drawing dots on to dry paper. Combining both techniques produced visual interest and an accurate description.

**C Scaly texture**
Small areas of light, regular cross-hatching with the water-soluble pencils suggest the scaly bodies of the fish. If this texture had been applied more extensively, it would have looked too mechanical.